# THE

# FOURTH LEVEL

Nature Wisdom Teachings

of the Inka

## Elizabeth B. Jenkins

International Bestselling Author

Back Cover Photo Credit: Dominique Jacot

*Note:* Most Quechua spellings are taken from the 1995 edition of the Quechua dictionary published by the Higher Academy of the Quechua Language, Cuzco, Peru.

Published in English by Pu'umaka'a Press

PO Box 500Naalehu, Hawaii 96772 USA

www.thefourthlevel.org

www.wiraqochafoundation.org

ISBN-10: 1491240903
ISBN-13: 978-1491240908

# DEDICATION

This book is dedicated with all my heart to the Paqos of the world, past, present, and future. May we all stand up as Pachamama Warriors promoting, protecting and enjoying the rights and the magnificence of MOTHER NATURE.

# CONTENTS

# ACKNOWLEDGMENTS

Foremost gratitude goes to my luminous guiding star, my gorgeous *Paqarina* and magnificent *Itu Apu.* Urpi Chai Sonqollay! For the super human beings in my life I am indebted beyond repay. For my *yanantin*, the most rugged manly man I know, Barney C. Frazier, thanks for being the veritable tower of power to whom I cling for stability when awash in the tidal flows of life. Thank you for your patience and humility. For five hundred years of resistance I give humble thanks and profound respect and gratitude to my beautiful compadres and comadres of the Q'ero Nation. To Juan Victor Nuñez del Prado Bejar, the veritable Joseph Campbell of the Andes, you saved my life! I am forever grateful and will always be your biggest fan. To Fredy Conde Huallpa, I praise your grandfather for training you in the path, and you for preserving and exemplifying the magnificence of your ancestors. Thanks to Karie Jacobson, editor extraordinaire, for smoothing the wrinkles in this manuscript.

Finally, to **ALL** the worldwide Paqos, your dedication to the fourth level simply makes life with living! When I think of you my heart overflows like a chocolate ñust'a fountain with kids sticking their fingers in. Ah yes…kids! To my beloved boys: my strong handsome and heartful Gabriel and my mischievous nymph like wild Sammy, you are my favorite people in the world. Thanks for letting me be your Mom and helping me write this book. My heart is open wide.

# INTRODUCTION

Now in this rather perilous moment in human history there IS a way out. I write this book offering hope of another tomorrow that can be achieved through the collective effort and collaboration of human beings with our supreme friend, guide, helper, teacher, chief cook and bottle washer…our ultimate Mother from whom all gifts spring…Great Nature. THE FOURTH LEVEL is a guide to a new way of being with Nature that arises from an ancient tradition and delivers itself to us here and now in the perfect moment of our greatest need. This is a wise and flexible tradition that holds no dogmas or rigid rules…only a series of invitations to *experience*. This kind of personal experience can save our lives. I know because it saved mine!

It has come to my attention that it is impossible to separate us humans from the geography in which we have organically grown. Each human cultures' wisdom, eyes, hair, and skin tone, is informed by the nature of the Nature of the geographic area in which we have developed over time. Not only the flora and fauna, but the living geography, the veritable spirit or consciousness of mountains, valleys, hillsides, streams, rivers, fjords, beaches, waterfalls, dunes, peninsulas, and caves near which we live affect us. It is the color of the air, quality of light, flavor of winds, and texture of cosmic vistas to which our geography grants us access, that has helped to shape our particular biological manifestation.

Our rather recent scientific discovery that race is non-existent, or rather that there is only one race, and that is Human, highlights this magnificent fact. Our rainbow colors are nothing more (and nothing less) than the amazing adaptation of our bodies to the natural environment in which we find ourselves evolving over time. This could mean that Nature has played a more unique role in our past evolution than we may have originally conceived. I put forth here in this book that our conscious participation with Nature will have a much greater impact on the future of human evolution than we could ever have guessed.

The mystical wisdom tradition of the Andes has maintained its' ceremonies and practices, philosophies and worldview and its' priesthood due to the fact that its' altars cannot be torn down. They are the very mountains, rivers, oceans, caves, streams and valleys in which we live. The Earth on which we walk is herself the altar. The principles of this tradition are formed upon the fundamental laws of physics. Nature herself is the teacher, the transmitter of energy and information. Infinitely generous, she proffers the open secret of her living energy upon all wise enough to grasp it. It has taken me years to understand this, and years to craft an explanation that could do justice to the beauty and awe this elegant, sophisticated native knowledge system inspires.

Over the past twenty-five years I have worked in this tradition primarily as a translator. Not a translator of language, but a "Chaka-Runa" a "bridge person," a translator between world views as divergent as planets. Since 1988 I have had the blessing, honor and privilege to closely associate with a culture of indigenous peoples living in the high Andes of Peru, now nearly extinct, who have retained a basic point of view much needed now by humankind. I will call this indigenous wisdom tradition Inka for simplicity. It includes the vast and glorious millennial wisdom of the ancient people of the Andes up to their culmination during the Inka Empire of the 16th century, and forward to their modern-day descendants, the Q'ero Indians of

Peru. These are a people who understand Nature, and the way in which we humans are related to it, in a manner that is staggering. It is my hope that the application of this knowledge will result in our deeper global collaboration with Nature through which we can provide ourselves, our children and grandchildren with what we all need most---a future.

# PREFACE

This book is a tool for the correction of perspective. Think of it as a much needed pair of glasses for the current myopia of our Western culture. If we adjust our viewpoint, all can be gained and nothing lost. Through 20 years of rubbing Bubbles with my beautiful humble friends, the Q'ero Indians of Peru, enough Q'ero has rubbed off on me to begin to rectify my perspective. I now understand the clear *primacy* of Nature. Throughout the cosmos (i.e., planets, galaxies, stars, moons, space) Nature is in far heftier abundance than human beings. She expresses significant intelligence for all to see. This holds true down here on this lovely sphere we call Mother Earth as well, humans are not, and have never been, primary.

We are *part* of a magnificent system of intelligent and creative design, together with many other species. We have simply not yet learned how to correctly play well together with them. I am certain our perspective can only be corrected from the inside out, and with our willing agreement. Thus this book contains Practices or 'Nature Contemplations' that are invitations to personal subjective experiences with the capacity to transform us. If we so choose, we can become what we truly are, more simple and wondrous than we ever could have imagined. The Inka Nature Wisdom in this book can open a path that allows us to travel willingly and willfully, sensuously and joyously, together laughing....to the Fourth Level.

My part has been one of learning to listen, trust and follow. Following the voice of Mother Nature has led my family to our fabulous home on the Big Island of Hawaii where we take care of our Organic Orchard, and where we founded the Hawaiian Headquarters for Wiraqocha Foundation in 2001. The Island has been a luscious cradle for our family and a loving nest for the growth of our beautiful sons Sammy and Gabriel. Generously she has lavished her bountiful nectar upon us all, in addition to sharing her poignant insights with me these past 12 years. Without her generosity I could not have written this book and for that beautiful Mother Hawaii I thank you and I am in your debt. Now, let me tell you about exactly where on earth, I am.

Hawai`i is the most remote place on our planet, surrounded in all directions by 2400 miles of magnificent Pacific Mother Ocean. Our lovely Island home has evolved over the past million years without any need for defensive plants or animals. This is the nature of her Nature. The island herself possesses and professes the deep ALOHA, the very spirit and undefended generosity of Mother Earth. The Big Island of Hawaii is the youngest in the island chain and, as the name suggests, the largest. She contains 11 of the 13 climate zones found on earth and 90% of her flora and fauna is endemic, meaning it exists nowhere else on earth. She is a mini Planet Earth.

A bit like the Q'ero, our Big Island Pachamama has evolved in isolation from the rest of the worlds' populations and this has preserved her special character, charm, wisdom, and the living energy in her very soil, trees, plants, insects, native birds, and animals, in her light, and air, and trade winds…all this that is her `aina. According to Inka Nature Wisdom the Hawaiian people would have been drawn here by energetic affinity, allowing the blending of their DNA with hers to bring about the Native Wisdom, the profound intelligence of the Hawaiian People, that engenders our deepest respect.

How can I explain my gratitude for the fortune that has brought me here, lazing in the lap of her tropical luxury, her fierce natural power, her profound intoxicating beauty? I have had twelve years to vibrate my bosons with hers, absorbing her unique earthly nectars—drinking from the unparalleled cosmic blaze of her Milky Way trailed heavens. And this has informed me.

Our farm, `Ai Lani Orchards (which means 'to eat heaven' or 'spiritual food' in Hawaiian) lies enveloped in the warm green folds of Mauna Loa, or 'long mountain,' truly the largest mountain on Earth by volume. She stands 14, 678 feet above the sea, with another 15,407 reaching to the ocean floor making her height a whopping 30,085 from sea floor to summit—taller than Mt. Everest! However, her gargantuan body depresses the sea floor another five miles, making her actual height a staggering 56,000 feet. Hawai`i Island is known as the "HEALING ISLAND" and indeed she is the perfect outpost from which to offer the Nature Wisdom teachings of the FOURTH LEVEL as she contains them in her very body.

When one feels rich to overflowing one is compelled to share. Thus I offer you these scenes and sounds of the Big Island, our Healing Island of Hawai`i, as the backdrop for the video version of these Seven Nature Contemplations, the Inka Practices of the Fourth level. These practices belong to the world. And now they belong to you.

# FOREWORD

When we exhale, a tree breathes in. When a tree exhales, we breathe in. I can't imagine being any more directly connected to nature than that example provides. Some time ago while producing my series Beyond Survival I found myself with Elizabeth Jenkins on the top of a mountain in Peru surrounded by a handful of Inkan elders. With these High Priests we sat together beside an icy pond, taking part in one of a dozen important ceremonies, meant to establish a connection between Mother Earth and ourselves.

As if on incredible, magical cue the weather performed and created and dissipated as the Q'ero Elders moved throughout the various parts of the ceremony. It seemed they moved the weather with a wave of their hands. For me, the participant, it was spell binding. And it was through the weather pattern that these High Priests determined my worthiness to continue. By the end of the week the Elders pulled me aside and said very solemnly and sternly that I will need to understand just how much power they had put into me. It was and is the power to connect on a spiritual, emotional, physical and energetic way with nature herself.

Elizabeth is no stranger to this powerful connection. It is in fact her life. And the time has come for Elders of the world to share their knowledge of connecting to the earth, before it is too late for our species survival. Elizabeth has so generously designed a concise road map for our souls and our physical and emotional selves to take, to lead us to peace and harmony on this planet. But what choice does she have? She, I am very sure, is compelled to do so. She is now burdened with this responsibility.

I share in her desires, to do through my music and my film work, what she can do with her words gleaned from years of direct experience with the masters of nature connectedness. Yet you don't need to go to Peru, or the jungles, or the Arctic or the deserts to experience this connection. Just go to the park on the corner, kick off your shoes, feel the earth and fall asleep against a tree and you will understand—that Elizabeth's writings and teachings are needed now more than ever. Desperately.

Les Stroud, Survivorman

# CHAPTER ZERO

## Our Human Right & Responsibility
## To Belong to the Natural World

The knowledge in this book is the birthright of every human being on earth. It is a guide to your own bliss experience; the bliss of being personally connected to nature and to feel like you belong in a way you may never have before. Perhaps this book will give you a completely new experience and understanding of who you are. Perhaps it will confirm what you have known all your life. In either case, the time you spend reading it and participating in the "Nature Contemplations" outlined here, will be time spent in BLISS...the bliss humans are designed to experience when we collaborate more fully with the forces of GREAT NATURE. And it is this bliss that shall mean our very survival.

There are people living now in our world who know how to speak directly with Nature and to collaborate with the climate...not in some spooky paranormal way, but in a wise adult human way. Shouldn't we all be wildly interested in their worldview and knowledge? In this age of toxic spills and climate change **this** is the wisdom we are missing.

Most of the knowledge I have gathered in this book comes through the grace and persistence of the Q'ero Indians of Peru—the modern-day descendants of the Inka. The Q'ero live in a remote area of the Andes in villages from 10,000 to 14,000 feet high and to the North East of Cuzco. They are an amazingly resilient, yet compassionate, soft-spoken, humble

1

people with enormous hearts (literally) and practical knowledge about natural living energy and healing. For a millennium they have practiced a way of being in relationship with Nature that is sacred, and preserved a knowledge system that I believe is now our key to human survival.

Yet this book could never have been written without the genius and enormous generosity of anthropologist Juan Victor Nuñez del Prado Bejar of Cuzco, Peru. Don Juan, my first Fourth Level teacher, began the work of translating the worldview of the Andean Mystical tradition in 1968. During the course of his research he met two of the few remaining Andean Masters of the Fourth-Level, whose knowledge thanks to Juan, flows throughout these pages. Juan is a rare treasure and, apart from the Q'ero themselves, the world's foremost authority on Q'ero culture and spiritual traditions—and all things Inka.

Since 1988, I have lived in Cuzco, city of the Inkas, for years at a time or spent months each year visiting many sacred areas, including the villages of the Q'ero Nation known as the "Last Inka Community" high in the Andean clouds. In Peru I acquired many non-ordinary experiences with the 'invisible world.' I also acquired many God-children. And in my twenty five years spent traveling back and forth to Peru I have grown to know and love some quite extraordinary people—farmers, moms, dads, community leaders, priests, healers, weather workers, "magicians," if you will. These 'regular folk' were capable of amazing things, a testament to the resources and capabilities of the human being.

With them and because of them, I witnessed things most people would consider 'impossible.' I am deeply grateful to have had my worldview turned upside down and inside out by my Andean friends, as well having the word "impossible" shattered and permanently deleted from my vocabulary. One of the best things I learned was that ordinary humans are capable of some quite extraordinary things—like collaborating with weather—and that this is possible for us all to learn.

The Inka prophecies declare that now is the time of the *Taripay Pacha* , the 'Age of Meeting Ourselves Again.' This time is marked by the global need for humanity to exchange all of our cultural achievements, a time when each human being is required to step forward into their destiny. We are growing from spiritual adolescence into spiritual adulthood. This time demands that we all begin to develop our individual and collective capacity for what we may currently think of as 'magic.'

> *MAGIC*: a supposed supernatural power that makes impossible things happen, or that gives somebody control over the forces of Nature...

Magic as defined by my dictionary accurately describes what some of our friends in Peru are capable of. However, they do not control Nature; they work **with** Her as friends and collaborators.

When my Q'ero friends blow on their coca leaves and we witness the clouds part, they are simply speaking with their friends...a technology we do not understand and therefore label as 'magic.' When we slide a plastic card into a wall and money comes out, they witness a technology they do not understand and therefore consider to be 'magic.' Now is the time for us to share our magic! NOW is the time for us all to step up and become the shamans or magicians we are capable of becoming and take our place of responsibility as adults.

However, because we were not raised in the High Andes

and given this knowledge along with our mother's milk, we must first make a few adjustments to our worldview. To do this we first have to understand Nature, not only from a scientific viewpoint—a highly crucial and vital gift of our modern era—but from a personal, intimate, subjective, and interactive viewpoint as well.

Our human quest to understand our relationship to nature has gone through many historical, cultural, and psychological transformations over the last few thousand years. We have gone from believing Nature to be a horrifying tyrant to whom we must sacrifice our children—to a terrible temptress against whom we must wage constant war—or to the current view (perhaps most heinous of all) in which Nature is nothing more than inert matter available for our unconscionable plundering. Over the centuries one thing is consistent— we have maintained a victim/perpetrator relationship with Nature, a relationship based in fear.

Fear of Nature has become the plague of our modern society. We live indoors in a virtual world of illusory control. Our loss of direct contact with Nature has led to a whole host of illnesses from physical to psychological to spiritual. Clearly we need Nature and cannot live without Her. This is the moment in which we must grow up our relationship with Nature to one of mutual intelligent respect, intimate personal connection, integrity, and life-sustaining collaboration. Our very survival depends on it!

On some level most of us know we love and need Nature, but do we know why? When we say something is natural; whether we are talking about food or describing a feeling state, situation or relationship, 'natural' almost always means good, right, easy, healthy or congruent! Conversely things that are "unnatural" feel wrong, uncomfortable, spooky, weird and creepy. But do we know why we like things that are natural? What is the nature of Nature? What and who are we in it? This book seeks to fuel the discussion and provide you direct experiences that will open new levels of understanding about our Human/Nature Relationship.

Why do we love nature? Perhaps because Nature provides something that we all need like food and shelter. But Nature also provides more intangible things like beauty....food for the soul. Have you ever noticed that Nature never ever makes a fashion mistake? She never puts two colors together that don't go. Her designs in plants, animals, and landscapes are always pleasing to us and magnificently efficient. She provides oxygen via her plants, trees, and forests....but surely you could go to an oxygen bar for that. Could there be something more? There must be. There is. And it has to do with energy.

Did you know that trees and plants not only produce oxygen for us but, according to the Q'ero Indians, they also produce a refined living energy, called *sami*—meaning nectar in the Inka language. This could be the explanation why we instinctively feel the need to go outside for a walk when we are grumpy. We are seeking *sami*, nature's nectar. This may also be the reason we feel better after we **do** go for a walk. Not only are we taking in oxygen but also a form of refined living energy that refreshes our whole being, our living energy system. How do we know this? Because the original scientists of this earth have taught us that it is so.

**science** [ˈsaɪəns] noun
the systematic study of the nature and behavior of the
material and physical universe, based on observation,
experiment, and measurement, and the formulation of laws
to describe these facts in general terms.
 --Merriam Webster's online dictionary


By our very definition of the term "science" we are
describing the activity of indigenous people over many
thousands of years before our word 'science' was ever
invented. It is only logical that our human ancestors who
most accurately observed and responded to the "behavior of
the material and physical universe" were the ones who
survived to pass on their genetic material. There is knowledge
held by indigenous wisdom keepers, keys to who we are, that
we have lost in the translation to our "modern" culture.

These key concepts form the way in which we
conceptualize ourselves—who we think we are—that directly
determines how we act. Therefore it is critical that we enlarge
our understanding of our human identity and learn how we
intertwine and collaborate with NATURE in the very core of
our beings in ways biological, psychological and spiritual. We
need this knowledge not only for the benefit of our everyday
lives, but to discover the direction of evolution for our species.
This direction, I propose, must be toward a much greater
collaborative harmony and participation with our fellow
species, and our entire ecosystem.

Not only is this shift in our viewpoint necessary for
our survival as a species, it is also a lot more fun! This fun is
not something that I am just going to tell you about it—I am
going to supply you methods…brilliant invitations devised by
this ancient tradition, leading to wonderful subjective
energetic experiences that allow you to feel and know this for

yourselves. Through two preparatory exercises and seven traditional Inka practices or "Nature Contemplations," included in this book, you will be given access to practices developed by a millennial wisdom tradition, guarded and maintained by a small group for centuries, and needed by all of us NOW! These exercises put us all firmly on the road to our own **energy independence**, increasing our Nature Intelligence (NQ—nature quotient), on a spiritual and personal, as well as collective level.

If you are a visual learner you can simply read the "Nature Contemplations" provided here with great descriptive detail, and practice them on your own. However if you happen to be an auditory learner like me, you may want to get the Seven (7) downloadable "guided contemplations" that have been made to accompany this book. For you visual types I made some lovely videos with fabulous Nature scenes from my home on the 'Healing Island' of Hawaii that accompany these guided meditations. My students worldwide have been asking me for years to make these recordings available. Finally, here they are.

Although the knowledge I have gathered in this book comes through the oral tradition of contemporary Inkas, let me point out that it is based in a philosophical framework shared by many indigenous peoples worldwide. In short, this is nothing new, but thanks to modern physics, and Albert Einsteins' equation relating matter and energy, we of the West are now finally poised to comprehend it. I present the information here in hopes that respect will follow closely on the heels of understanding.

By now most of us are aware through science and the advents of modern physics that our understanding of "the

7

physical universe" (i.e., nature) has developed to include the simple and profound notion that everything is living energy. From the tiniest measurable particles that spin on their own axis (just like our planet), to our cells, to our bodies, to our children, homes and families, our villages, cities, and countries, our rivers, forests, mountains, oceans, all our ecosystems, our planet as a whole, our solar system, even our galaxy and our universe are all made of living energy.

What we don't yet know is how to participate consciously within that energy universe. This book is an effort to teach us how we can participate with living energy from elementary particles to our own energy Bubbles, to the living fusion reactor that is our Sun.

The application of this real knowledge based in scientific fact; that we, and everything in our world is made of living energy, puts the power to influence our world directly into our hearts and hands. This book is a guide to help you use that knowledge to empower yourself as a happy, harmonious, self-responsible, and self-directed bee in the garden of humanity.

Below I present Seven Principles of the Inka Energy World; principles that must be experienced to be understood. This is why each principle comes with a practice, or experiential exercise. The explanation of these principles is offered here to describe and convey an organic framework about the world of living energies....how it works, and how we can play with it. Just so you know what's coming, every successive chapter of this book will further elaborate one principle with real life examples, and the chapter will end with an experiential exercise so that, should you so choose, you can have your own direct visceral experience of the principle.

These principles are my attempt to communicate the

marvelous Andean worldview. I invite you to consider them, try them on and enjoy them. Don't see them as any religious or spiritual dogma. Rather understand them as the next global out-flowering of knowledge about who we are as human beings, what we can do as a result of how we define ourselves, and how this can help us realize our most important birth rights: health, happiness, harmony, responsibility, love, power, beauty and magic.

I invite all to **play** with this system engaging your perceptive minds, and discerning hearts, to determine if it works for you as it has for me, and many others. The intention of this book is dedicated to making this vital sacred knowledge universally accessible because, I believe, it is our human right. So please just sit back and enjoy the wisdom and exercises provided here for your nourishment.

# SEVEN PRINCIPLES OF THE LIVING ENERGY WORLD

## 1: KAWSAY PACHA: THE LIVING ENERGY WORLD

EVERYTHING IS IN OUR WORLD IS ALIVE and possesses both a physical and energetic aspect: molecules, cells, fish, humans, trees, cars, rivers, buildings, mountains, cities, oceans, planets, stars. Our cosmos is overflowing with a superabundance of finest living energy and we have a human right to receive it.

## 2. AYNI: SACRED EXCHANGE

Energy follows thought and moves and flows by natural reciprocal exchanges. As human beings we come equipped with the ability to receive and direct living energy through our intention. Trust makes energy flow, doubt inhibits the flow. We are biologically, psychologically, and spiritually designed to collaborate with Mother Nature and these sacred reciprocal exchanges are the basis of life, i.e., BREATHING!

## 3. YANANTIN: HARMONIOUS RELATIONSHIP BETWEEN COMPLEMENTS

*Yanantin* philosophy is the celebration of difference. All differences are beneficial and complementary, male/female, hot/cold, night/day, heavy/fine. Living energy is neither positive nor negative, rather it is 'heavy' or 'fine'. All energy is useful. Collaborative exchange of differences is life affirming.

## 4. INKA MUJU (ENERGY SEED): QOSQO/SACRED CENTER

Everything from to cells to animals to human bodies to cities to planets to Galaxies have a central digestive system—that is both physical and energetic. We humans can activate and co-operate with this system to create health and well being in ourselves, families, cities, nations. Within our sacred center lies our Inka Seed that holds the Seven Levels of our complete human potential.

## 5. IRRIGATION OR ENERGY TRIGGER

Qarpay literally means irrigation or watering in Quechua. Used in the ritual sense it is an energetic transmission of living energy between Nature and humans that triggers our psycho-spiritual growth to the next level. Qarpay is the irrigation of our Inka Seed that softens the hard outer casing to allow the possibility of spiritual sprouting. The Seven Energy Eyes (Ñawis) of our body open to connect with the five primary living energies of Nature.

## 6. WIÑAY: ENERGETIC GERMINATION OF OUR SACRED IDENTITY

Our energetic connection to the *TEQSE* (global) *Apus* through our Energy Eyes stimulates the potential of our Inka Seed to germinate. *Chumpi Away* is the Inka practice by which we weave our energy belts, connecting 'Energy Eye' to 'root,' in order to strengthen our Bubble and establish harmonious relationships with our larger natural and energetic environment. We sprout our Sacred Identity by locating and incorporating the natural energies of our *Paqarina* (nature Mom), *Itu Apu* (nature Dad) and Guiding Star. This empowers our Bubble with the requisite living energy to flower forth to our destiny.

## 7. PHUTUY: ENERGETIC FLOWERING

Culmination of our Fourth-Level practice occurs through the nourishment of our Inka Seed, our sacred identity, with the living energies of the Five Nectars to bring about spiritual 'flowering.' This prepares us to practice the ultimate *Qarpay*

*Ayni* that marks the beginning of the collective energy practices. We continue our evolution through the seven levels of psychospiritual development that take us on a journey of ever-deeper collaboration with Nature's larger living systems

# CHAPTER ONE

# EVERYTHING IS ALIVE!

## Principle 1. *KAWSAY PACHA*: THE NATURAL LIVING ENERGY WORLD

**EVERYTHING IN OUR WORLD IS ALIVE and possesses both a physical and energetic aspect: molecules, cells, people, fish, trees, cars, rivers, buildings, mountains, cities, oceans, planets, stars. Our cosmos is overflowing with a superabundance of finest living energy and we have a human right to receive it.**

*"Look deep, deep into nature, and then you will*

*understand everything better."*

---Albert Einstein

For the past two centuries most of us have been raised in a society that believed in the primacy of matter. We have been taught the material world is the only one worth talking or thinking about, in fact that it is the only world that exists. But now we have scientific evidence, reason to believe, that another worldview may be more accurate—one is which energy is primary and perhaps in some ways, more fundamental than matter. So what if that was true? How does that change my day?

In this chapter I shall champion the idea that not only are we and everything in Nature (indeed *everything*) made of living energy, but that we have a human right to personally experience and enjoy this Natural World of Living Energy. Further, that this direct personal interaction with Nature can make us a happier, healthier and more harmonious people and society.

## NATURE IS LIVING ENERGY

Science, in its early phases, seemed to tell us that our Earth was composed of mostly lifeless matter, and that we ourselves were mere biological machines. As science progressed however, we witnessed the advent of modern physics, and Albert Einstein's equation relating matter and energy, that expanded our notion of what our universe is made of.

Our understanding has indeed transformed with Einstein's famous equation E=mc squared. Modern physics has delved into the most staggering implications of that little equation. If we believe Einstein that E (energy) really does equal mc 2 (mass times the speed of light squared) then we are agreeing that mass, matter and energy are incontrovertibly related. There can be no mass or matter without energy. From the tiniest measurable particles that spin on their own axis (just like our planet), to our cells, to our bodies, to our children, homes and families, our villages, cities, and countries, our rivers, forests, mountains, oceans, even our galaxy and our universe – all are made of living energy.

With the recent preliminary evidence of the Higgs

boson proving the Higgs field, there is now little doubt that everything is made of living energy. To prove the existence of the Higgs field is brilliant, but to understand how humans participate with living energy just could be considered genius! And that is where our Andean friends come in.

The simple and profound notion that everything is living energy means that *nothing* in our material universe is dead. Again, this concept is not really new – in fact, it is ancient. Many spiritual traditions around the world have defined terms for the energetic component of our universe. Hawaiians call it *Mana;* Hindus, *Prana.* It is *Ki* in Japanese, *Qi* or *Chi* in Chinese. Tibetan Buddhists call living energy *Leung,* Druids call it *nwyfre,* and in the Mexica tradition it is called *teotl.* Western mystics call living energy 'life force,' or simply 'consciousness,' and in the immensely popular Star Wars movies, it is called "The Force." The Andean people call it *Kawsay* (pronounced cow-sigh) that also translates as 'life' or 'health' in Quechua, and you can see *Kawsay Clinica* (health clinic) signs all over the Andes.

It would seem that our science has finally caught up with what indigenous people around the world have known for millennia, that everything is alive. Even our Western culture recognizes that this life force has 'consciousness.' We have only to observe the activity in a forest, feel the pulsing ocean, or stare at the blaze of fiery stars in the night sky to recognize that Nature is a source of living energy. According to Inka wisdom, everything is part of the *Kawsay Pacha,* the world of living energies. But for the Andeans she is much more than that.

There is a saying in Peru: "Fruits are the kisses of *Pachamama* (Mother Earth)." In this view, a loving and generous Mother Earth has offered us the gift of life in this beautiful world. Thus, our only attitude could be one of great humility and thankfulness toward the Natural world that sustains us. Certainly no one can argue that Mother Earth provides us with our every need. But are we generous enough to afford Nature her own form of consciousness? How would it change our relationship to her if we did?

Now let's take the discussion home. What happens if we take it a step further and actually live as if we ARE matter and energy?

## WE ARE MADE OF LIVING ENERGY

We ourselves are not merely made of bones, blood, and muscle, but of energy. Now we can even measure the living energy we possess via specific instrumentation. EKG's (electrocardiograms) measure electrical energy in the heart and EEG's (electroencephalogram) measure electrical energy in the brain. When people go into a coma we actually define whether they are living or dead by the amount of electrical activity measurably present in their brains.

The highly sensitive instrument called the SQUID (superconducting quantum interference device) magnetometer can accurately and reliably measure not only the specific energy field of each organ of the body, but the energy field of our entire physical body as well. The SQUID magnetometer is the technology inside instruments like MRI's (magnetic resonance imaging) used in hospitals to look inside the human body to help diagnose. The same instrumentation is also used in the gyroscopes of Gravity Probe B in outer space, in a project designed by NASA and Stanford University to test the limits of Einstein's general theory of relativity.

There are even scientific studies to prove the existen(
of that invisible energetic part of the human being we call the
soul. Controlled scientific studies of dying people offer a
measurable 'weight of the soul,' -- that part that leaves our
bodies when we die. Our soul has consistently been measured
by modern scientific researchers at the Institute of Noetic
Sciences, (1988) to weigh 1/3000th of an ounce, an
experiment corroborated by German researchers.

Contemplate the fact that you are made of living
energy.

How we define ourselves has an enormous impact on our
lives. Who we think we are defines how we behave – and
what we can and cannot achieve. Let me offer a simple,
personal example. Prior to 1994, being an author was not in
any way part of my identity, nor did I think it would ever be.
In order to allow the possibility, I had to go through a rather
painful personal process to expand my concept of who I was.
Three books later, I can say I effectively integrated "author" as
part of my identity, and this has helped open my life to
fascinating new experiences.

When we enlarge our understanding of our human
identity, we open ourselves to new experiences and new
abilities, and new possibilities. Acknowledging that we are
made of matter and energy is a first step. Once we realize
what we are made of, we can open ourselves to these
experiences, and begin to discover what we are capable of.

Since we humans and everything else; i.e., trees, rivers,
oceans, mountains, planets, solar systems and galaxies, are all
made of living energy, then we share a common basis. In fact
it is through this common energetic basis that we can

'communicate' with everything around us. Therefore there must be principles governing the interaction of the living energy of which all is made, that human beings can learn about, practice, and apply to the benefit of all.

## THE HUMAN-NATURE CONNECTION

Most of us know that we love Nature. We innately look up to Nature as a larger living system with an ingenious design that is life sustaining and life affirming. Psychologist Erich Fromm first used the term "biophilia"--literally meaning love of life or living systems--to describe a psychological orientation of being attracted to all that is alive and vital.

Harvard biologist Edward O. Wilson uses the term in the same sense, when he suggests that our "biophilic instinct'" describes "the connections that human beings subconsciously seek with the rest of life." He proposed the possibility that the deep affiliations we humans have with Nature are rooted in our biology. Evolutionary psychology suggests that our biophilic instinct nudges us along to *connect with larger living systems* as the direction of our evolution. Inka wisdom further suggests that this larger living system is out there, patiently waiting for us to figure out how to connect.

Unfortunately, there are some in our culture who are "bio phobic," - fearful of Nature. My husband and I are organic farmers with an open-air roadside Fruit Stand, and we continually bear witness to this modern malady. There are many people who stop at our stand yet don't want to get out of their car for fear that Nature might touch them.

Most people, however, *love* Nature, and kids usually just can't help themselves! The biophilic folks (a much larger percentage of our customers) rush out of their cars to breathe the clean air, to touch the living fruit still ripening on the trees in front of them, and to take in the peace, beauty, tranquility and productivity of our orchards. We naturally want to connect with Nature because we are unconsciously seeking the reciprocal exchange of living energies that is so biophilic.

In order to exchange with Nature you have to give and receive. To receive you must relax and be open…and this implies trust. It's lucky that breathing is autonomic or many bio phobes might end up dead - not trusting the plants and the trees! Trust makes energy flow. Doubt inhibits flow.

To illustrate the concept that human beings and Nature are deeply designed to collaborate, let's look at the fundamental act of breathing. We humans breathe in oxygen created for us by plants, trees, seaweed, algae, and marine phytoplankton, and we breathe out carbon dioxide, which is life's breath for them. This supremely mutually beneficial exchange is the basis on which our moment-to-moment life is sustained. We can live for a bit without food and water, but cut off our oxygen and very shortly we are "pushing up daisies"… so to speak.

If you were a Q'ero you would have grown up knowing and believing that Nature produces finest living energy for us with much love. According to the Q'ero, with every breath we take, we are experiencing a sacred exchange with Nature, and not only in the form of exchanging carbon dioxide for oxygen. The Q'ero tell us that trees, plants and other living beings not only produce oxygen for us but also produce a refined living energy, called *sami*, meaning 'nectar' in the Quechua language.

I have come to believe this IS the explanation why we feel the need to go outside when we are grumpy. We instinctively seek *Sami*, natures' nectar for our healing and well-being. We feel better when we go for a hike or go sit by the ocean because it gives us the ineffable something that takes our stress away. Why? Because all of nature constantly emits this living energy the Inkas call *sami*. And this nectar refreshes us down to our bosons. *Sami,* the finest living energy of Nature, makes us healthy and keeps us happy. And Nature's *sami* comes in many different flavors, as you will see.

Nectar is just one term of many that reflects the genius of the Andean people and the Quechua language for developing its' rich vocabulary to describe human experiences of living energy.

With their permission, I am going to borrow some of their language to use throughout this book.

## THE LIVING ENERGY FIELD or BUBBLE

*Poq'po,* pronounced poke-poh, means bubble in the native Andean language of the Inkas, Quechua. This is the term the Andean Masters use for the energy field surrounding each of us. The *Poq'po* is similar to what some call the aura, and others call the electromagnetic field or the human energy field.

Bubble is a wonderfully appropriate and visual word for describing the human energy field. A bubble's shape clearly defines a boundary. It is transparent yet can contain. Most importantly, Bubble is not a human-centric term, as it can describe equally the field of living energy around a human being, a river, a city, or a star. Everything – every human, all of Nature, in fact every single thing in the universe - possesses a Bubble. It is something we all share in common.

Your Bubble has sensations and perceptions that you can pay attention to, just as you can pay attention to the sensations and perceptions of your physical body. I am about to teach you how to pay attention to those perceptions with some beginning exercises.

If you ever have the blessing to meet some of my Andean friends from the villages of Q'eros, you will notice that they are very calm, gentle, and trusting. They trust *Pachamama* -Mother Earth - and they trust their own experience. Let me illustrate with an example.

In September 1996, Wiraqocha Foundation invited two young Q'ero priests to Redlands University in California to teach their knowledge. During the campus tour we entered the library where at the front door, one of the young priests stopped, astounded at the sight of a six-foot globe. "This is a model of Pachamama," we told him. Having never before seen a globe, he spent several long minutes circling it while exclaiming in wonder and amazement, "of course...of course." Finally he said to us "No wonder the *Mama Qocha* (Mother Ocean) is SO powerful when you call her...look how big she is!"

This experience remedied a conundrum for young Don Augustin Pauqar Ccapac, as the only bodies of water he had seen growing up were relatively small glacial lakes. His first and only experience of the ocean occurred when flying over it from Peru to California. However, this young man's knowledge of the power of Water had come through his direct experience of calling upon her living energy. Seeing the globe of the Earth at last explained what he had already perceived directly on an energetic level.

The education of a Q'ero is in stark contrast to the way we typically receive knowledge about our Earth and ourselves. We are often merely memorizing knowledge told to us by someone else, and experiential knowledge comes later, if ever.

What I am going to ask you to do now, flies in the face of probably most, if not all, of your education and training. I am going to ask YOU to be the expert on your own experience. You are the only one who knows what you perceive through your own Bubble. Trust makes energy flow. Doubt inhibits the flow. I am going to ask you to look to yourself as 'expert' and allow your inner experience to predominate. In this book we are going to educate you like a Q'ero. You are the boss of your own Bubble.

The following preparatory exercises will allow you to experience the Inka worldview for yourself. (In Chapter Two, we will move into the first true Inka Practices, which I present as taught by my Andean teachers.)

Energy is information, and each of us has a unique way to receive the information coming to us from the living energy world. Our various learning styles (some of us are visual, some kinesthetic, some auditory, etc.) will probably influence our modes of perceiving living energy. Some of us are very good at perceiving living energy, just as some of us are innately better at art or music. But don't worry, all of us can improve with practice.

If you are a visual learner, you can simply read the 'Nature Contemplations' provided here, and practice them on your own. I have also provided some illustrations and diagrams for your viewing pleasure. If you happen to be an auditory learner, you may want to listen to the seven (7) downloadable guided "Nature Contemplations" that accompany this book. My students worldwide have been asking me for years to make these recordings available. Finally, here they are. As a musician and a highly auditory learner myself, I found the recordings a lot of fun to make. I think they will be of enormous value to all of you auditory learners out there. We decided to include some beautiful scenery from Hawaii. So for those of you who wish, you have an option to get the Nature Contemplations as video clips as well.

Though I urge you to explore your own style of learning when doing these exercises, please don't be a perception "imperialist." In other words refrain from disavowing an information channel because you don't think it's the "correct" one. This is where expectation can get in the way of perception. Perceptual prejudice is actually quite common. Our culture on the whole has a bias toward frontal visual information; hence we say, "seeing is believing." Therefore I invite you to practice without prejudice for or against any one perceptual channel. Allow information to come in to you as it naturally does, without favoring any one mode of perception.

Here and now I invite you to practice paying attention. This is completely up to you, but I warn you - this is the *really* fun part of this book.

Go outside, or you can stay inside if you prefer. It doesn't matter, energy doesn't mind! However, I will describe this as if you are outside because it is easier and more fun for me. Hopefully it is a nice sunny day with a bit of a breeze and a few clouds and you have a lovely natural body of water near at hand, but again, it is not required. Your Bubble can reach everywhere via your intention.

## Preparatory exercise #1: *KAWSAY PACHA*

## EXPERIENCE THE WORLD AS LIVING ENERGY

Standing outside in the green grass, take a moment to open your awareness to the possibility that you and everything around you is living energy. Take some nice deep breaths and enjoy this for a moment. Notice your breathing and calm your attention until you can perceive the beating of your own heart. Pay attention to the natural functioning of your body and if you wish, say "thank you" to all your organs and your autonomic nervous system for all it does. Spend some moments appreciating this rare opportunity to be alive.

Next, feel the life force rushing all through your body from your beating heart. Experience yourself as physical matter, bones, blood, muscle, organs...*and* as living energy. Bring your awareness to your own personal energy Bubble. Notice its texture, flavor, sound, color, and smell. Pay attention to your own personal field of living energy surrounding and interpenetrating your physical body and extending beyond it. Enjoy this, it is yours - your Bubble. And YOU are Bubble boss!

Remember, each of us perceives best through different sensory channels. Any way *you* do it is the *correct* way. Allow yourself a few adjectives to describe the texture, taste, feeling, and sensory experience of the living energy that is you. Perceive it directly. Let your mental "knowledge" remain in the background. Let yourself sense or feel primarily with your direct perception. Your Bubble normally extends about an arms length out in all directions.

Now, simply extend your Bubble (your awareness) toward the earth and perceive (sense, taste, smell, hear, intuit) the earth as living energy, and Mother Earth as one entire living being. Take a few moments to ENJOY this perception. Ahhhhh...

Now bring your awareness back close to your body, back to your own personal Bubble. Extend your Bubble again, this time towards the sun, and perceive the Sun's living energy. This is a relatively easy one as we can actually feel the warmth of the Sun's energy on our faces. We can see and feel it when this energy warms up our world in the morning and brings out the colors. It's really not much of a stretch for us to think of our Sun as living energy, but how about thinking of the Sun as a living being? Extend the experiment to perceive Sun energy directly through your Bubble and perceive 'Father Sun' as a living being rather than an object or 'thing,' or 'ball of gas.' Perceive the living energy of the being that is the Sun. Enjoy this and allow yourself a few adjectives to describe the flavor or sensation of it. Bring your attention back to your own Bubble.

Extend your awareness this time towards the body of Water is closest to you. This could be a vast ocean, river, a lake, a small stream, pond, or spring. If there is no body of water near you, extend your awareness to the groundwater that exists almost everywhere beneath our feet. Perceive this water body as living energy. Perceive the most refined essence of the Water, it's 'sami.' Enjoy this perception of the living being that is the Mother Water and of all of the life that she contains. Allow yourself a few adjectives to describe your perception of the living spirit of Water. Bring your awareness back to your own Bubble.

Now, extend your Bubble again, this time to the Wind, whose

activity can be wild or exceedingly subtle. Perceive the Wind as living energy. Enjoy the Wind as a living being. Then bring your attention back to your own Bubble.

Now compare these finest living energies or 'nectars' of SUN, EARTH, WATER, and WIND. Can you feel, taste, smell, sense, hear, the unique flavors and textures of these living energies? Can you sense the diverse qualities of these sources of living energy? Are you a solid enough citizen to allow them to be living beings with their own form of consciousness, rather than objects or things put here for "man's use"?

You can try this experiment with every single aspect of your world. Experience a rainbow as living energy, a stand of trees, a waterfall, or a mountain.

If your reaction to this, your own personal subjective experience with the above techniques, is to say, "Oh but I only imagined all that," I want you to ponder this next quote from our dear friend Albert:

> *"I'm enough of an artist to draw freely on my imagination. Imagination is more important than knowledge. Knowledge is limited; imagination encircles the world."*

> --Albert Einstein

If other insights or inspirations come to you, write them down. If you receive communications from the plants and trees, write, sing, or draw them if you wish. Keep a journal or log of your "Nature Communications."

Continue to do this every day for one week and take note of the immediate and secondary benefits you experience. Keep a log of your experiences. You are learning the simple joy of our personal subjective life-affirming collaboration with Nature as it was originally intended. When you are ready, move on to Preparatory Exercise #2.

## Preparatory Exercise # 2 -BREATHING!

Can understanding more about what we are breathing in and out literally change or enhance our experience of breathing? Of course it can. Breathing, our most basic biological function, the most fundamental act of our autonomic nervous system, is in fact a sacred exchange with Nature. How can experiencing that NOT make you smile?

Find yourself a relaxed spot without any cell phones ringing or televisions hooting at you, or any other potential interruptions. If possible take a seat on some nice green grass in a quiet garden somewhere.

Now, focus your attention on your physical body, beginning to relax and pay attention to your more subtle perceptions and feelings. Allow your attention to pass over your physical body, taking an inventory of the sensations you find there. Take time to pay attention to the autonomic function of your heart, and to your breathing. Did you know that when detoxifying your body approximately *seventy percent* of detoxification occurs through breathing? Clearly, breathing is supremely important. Once you feel very relaxed and tuned in to your own body, allow your intention to move to your Bubble, the field of living energy surrounding and interpenetrating your physical body. Take a moment to perceive yourself as physical substance; feel your body sitting against the chair. Tune in to your Bubble. Enjoy your own personal energy Bubble's flavor and texture.

Now, take a moment to expand your awareness to perceive all the plants and trees around you. Perceive them as living energy as well. You may begin to hear the sounds of Nature near you....a bird or a cricket singing...a dog or a stream or breeze...a bee buzzing away at its job. Take your time, and acknowledge them as living beings cohabitating with you on our lovely living planet. You can certainly see, feel, hear, or perceive them, and, each in their own way can see, feel, and perceive you too.

Now as you pay finer attention to your breathing, extend your Bubble out to greet the trees and plants around you. You might notice for the first or the hundredth time that trees and plants are benevolent entities. By simply doing their thing, they are providing innumerable benefits - they are affirming life. Certainly, they would still make oxygen with or without you sitting there. But you ARE sitting there.

As you breathe in their delicious gift of live-giving oxygen, open yourself to receive their finest living energy, their nectar, their love that they extend to you so freely.

As you exhale, form an intention to exhale love and gratitude back to them in return, along with your carbon dioxide. Send your love out to touch all the trees and plants around you. Say "thank you" for the gift of being alive and for experiencing this moment.

When you breathe in, receive the finest energy – finest nectar – finest love - along with the oxygen that the plants and trees are making for you. Continue to exhale love and gratitude along with your carbon dioxide toward the plants and trees. Equally continue to inhale the finest living energy of the trees and plants along with the oxygen you are receiving. Say 'thank you' as you breath in, and thank you as you breathe out.

Thanks for making me oxygen, thanks for taking my carbon dioxide.

This is the same breathing you have always been doing your whole life - just made infinitely more conscious and celebratory.

Receive the love the plants are offering along with their oxygen. Offer love in return along with your carbon dioxide. Enjoy the energetic connection you feel with Nature as you do this.

Continue to do this until you feel a sense of connection and harmony between you and the trees and plants around you, between you and your immediate environment. Continue until you feel a sense of well being inside you and outside you, a feeling of collaboration. The plants and trees are pointing toward something else...something bigger. They are showing us what to do. They too are biophilic, and their attention is directed toward receiving the nectar of a larger living system – the sun. They live not only from our life-giving carbon dioxide, but from drinking in the life-giving rays of the Sun as well. So be like the trees...open your leaves....collect the light. Open your Bubble and receive the nectar. When we do this together everything becomes right. Open your leaves. Collect the light!

If your eyes are closed, open them. Notice...has your visual experience changed? Does the world look different? Notice if your subjective experience has changed. Do you feel different? If so, how? Write it down.

Notice if you feel better in any way than you did prior to performing this exercise. Jot down your notes about your own experience.

Congratulations! You have just participated in the most primordial of all sacred exchanges with Nature.

Now you are better prepared to comprehend the next key concept of the Inka Wisdom Tradition, and the topic of Chapter Two –*Ayni,* or Sacred Exchange.

# CHAPTER TWO

# SACRED EXCHANGE

## Principle 2. *AYNI*, SACRED EXCHANGE

**Energy follows thought and moves and flows by natural reciprocal exchanges. As human beings we come equipped with the ability to receive and direct living energy through our intention. Trust makes energy flow, doubt inhibits the flow. We are biologically, psychologically, and spiritually designed to collaborate with Mother Nature and these sacred reciprocal exchanges are the basis of life, i.e., breathing!**

*"In the world of the quantum particle, fields are created by exchanges of energy....all elementary particles interact with each other by exchanging energy."*

--Lynne McTaggart, author of *The Intention Experiment*

The Quechua word *Ayni* translates as "Sacred Reciprocity," or Sacred Exchange. This is one of the most important principles of the Inka worldview. Ayni is the only real rule or law of the Inka Wisdom Tradition. The Law of *Ayni* is simple yet profound. It can be summed up in the following sentence: when you receive, you must give, and when you give, you must receive.

In the last chapter, you experienced that the very act of breathing is *Ayni*. There are many other examples of biological exchanges with Nature that are beneficial to us. Plants not only provide oxygen, but also clean the air of harmful toxins. How kind of them! Did you know that Peace Lilies not only produce oxygen for us, but also remove benzene, formaldehyde, acetone, ammonia and trichloroethylene from the air? These are all toxins that we produce by making the synthetic stuff we use in our houses, like carpets. How convenient Nature has made a houseplant that is not only beautiful, but can get rid of these toxic substances for us! Nature shows her alchemical ability once again when processing animal waste, that enriches the soil in which food is grown, as well as disseminating seeds from plants, which, in their turn, grow into more food—helping both humans and Nature. Like the breathing exchange, Nature is Queen at providing 'win-win' opportunities.

What an excellent bargain Nature gives us: we exchange our waste for something of incredible value, like oxygen or food. In economic terms, that would be a gold return on your 'pooh' investment every time! If Nature could embody herself and walk into our corporate offices, tell me what corporate executives would not be rolling out the red carpet and giving the VIP treatment to a partner so beneficial to our business of living? The best part about it is that both sides feel they are getting gold in exchange for waste. Getting rid of something you really don't want in exchange for something you can't live without is a deal anyone would love.

In the Inka point of view Nature is considered intelligent and largely benevolent as long as one keeps up one's end of the law of sacred reciprocity with her. Exchanging energies with Nature is considered not only our human *right,* but also our human *responsibility.* Clearly whether or not carbon dioxide or oxygen is 'good' or 'bad' depends on what side of the exchange you are on, just like with living energy. So in order to exchange living energy properly and freely we must cease to think in terms of 'good' and 'bad' energies, or 'positive' and 'negative' energies, as these terms are simply inaccurate descriptions of the energy world.

Now that you have practiced how to perceive the world as living energy, and experienced the exchange of energies that is our breathing, it's time to get going and learn how to direct living energy.

The Andean Masters say that humans can "drive the Kawsay" (move energy or affect reality) by using the "three powers" of the human being. The first is *Yachay,* the power of the mind. *Second is Llank'ay,* the power of the body or of getting things done in the material plane. And third is *Munay,* a beautiful Quechua word which means, "the human power of love and will used together." Put another way, *Munay* is directed love or intentional love. We use our *Munay* to move living energy.

We exchange living energies with our world all the time. Now the fun is to do this with a little more awareness and above all—intention. Energy follows thought and intention directs energy. Remember that energy is information, and because energy follows thought, so we direct living energy by applying our will through our intention.

*Munay* is the high and noble meaning of our word 'intention.' In the two traditional Inka Practices presented in this chapter, we will use our *Munay* to move energy in collaboration with Great Nature.

We are concerned here with what can be accomplished through blending our energies with the larger living systems of Nature in a biophilic life-affirming manner. There is no need to invent these flows of energy, we are simply learning how to collaboratively move along with flows of Nature that are already happening. When we add our intention, our *munay*, we increase the flow, participating in the movements of a larger energy system, and thus bringing deeper meaning to the saying "go with the flow!"

If I intend to phone my friend, my will is already moving energy in her direction, even before my arm moves towards my phone or my finger towards dialing her number. Haven't you sometimes known who was calling before you answered your phone? Their intention has flowed energy in your direction and if your Bubble is open, you may be able to receive their energy and therefore perceive the contact from them even before the phone rings.

One day when my son Sam was about six years old, we were sitting at the kitchen table eating lunch. Suddenly he looked up and said, "Mom, who's Almeta?" About twenty seconds later the phone rang and it was my husband's Aunt Almeta, whom we hadn't spoken to in more than six months! Kids are particularly good at receiving energy because their Bubbles aren't all clogged up yet; their perception is clearer.

The *Kawsay Pacha* or Energy World of the Inkas is divided into three layers distinguished by the quality of living energy in each. *Hanaq Pacha* refers to the "Upper World" or what we may think of as "heaven," and is filled with finest living energy called *sami*, or nectar. Hanaq Pacha is inhabited by refined beings.

*Kay Pacha* refers to the "Middle World," our earth or the world of material consciousness, inhabited by human as well as Nature Beings such as Mountain and River spirits. *Kay Pacha* contains a mix of heavy and fine energies.

*Ukhu Pacha* is the Lower or Inner World.  It may be

natural to assume that *Ukhu Pacha* is parallel to the Western notion of "hell," but *Ukhu Pacha* is **very** different from "hell." It is closer to the concept of the unconscious, and refers to the inside of ourselves as well as the inside of the earth. Think of it as a place of more gravity to which heavy energies naturally want to flow. It is inhabited by denser energies and heavier beings.

Remember, we discussed in the previous chapter how Nature emits a refined energy called *sami*. The complementary energy to *sami* is called *hoocha*, or heavy energy.

Heavy and fine energies need to be continually moved or 'flowed' to the right place to produce their natural and beneficial effects. And it is up to us humans to do it. We need to routincly release (give or offer) heavy energy in order to maintain health, just as we must release bodily wastes and we must exhale carbon dioxide. And, for optimum health, we humans need to ingest fine energy on a regular basis, just as we need fresh oxygen, food and water.

When I greet my Hawaiian friends we don't kiss or hug first; we put our foreheads together and *honi*. That means to breathe in each other's *ha* (breath of life.) We are exchanging energy Bubbles because it is considered a mutually beneficial life-affirming practice.

For the Q'ero (like Hawaiians and most indigenous folks) the clean-ness of one's Bubble or "spiritual hygiene" is of supreme importance. You will find their Bubble hygiene is impeccable. Many Western people have stated a feeling of wanting to be around them because of the sweetness and calmness and cleanness of their Bubbles.

If, like the Q'ero or Hawaiians, you might bump into

friends with whom you will exchange your living energy, you will want to keep your Bubble clean and shiny. After all, it's only polite; like showering or brushing teeth, but on an energetic level.

Energy is like water; it cleans itself out through movement. Just like energy, water is not "good' or 'bad' but can be 'clean' like sami or dirty like "hoocha.' Just as water is not 'negative' or 'evil,' neither is energy. In order to exchange energy properly we must stop thinking of energy as 'negative' or 'positive' and know that it is kept clean through movement.

We must facilitate the circulation or movement of energy through organic reciprocal exchanges to keep all systems healthy.

*Saminchakuy* (pronounced sah-meen-chah-khwee) and *Saywaychakuy* (sigh-wah-chah-khwee) are the traditional Inka Practices of circulating finest energies of Earth and Cosmos. These practices are one of the reasons why the Q'ero Indians always seem so happy and relaxed. They regularly engage in circulating energies through the *Kawsay Pacha,* the Living Energy World, via certain ceremonial practices that enhance our Human to Nature energy exchanges, just like breathing.

The simple practice of *Saminchakuy,* receiving refined energy of the Cosmos and releasing heavy energy to Mother Earth, provides great benefit to everyone who practices this.

I am reminded of one of our younger Paqos who had been actively suicidal from twelve years of age. This young person had experienced a life filled with family pain and trauma that no amount of therapy or depression medication was able to relieve. Once he discovered there was somewhere (Mother Earth) to which he could release his heavy energy and all his pain and suffering, his life dramatically improved. He has gone on to be a truly happy, life-affirming person in his job and his community.

The Andean Masters say that even using only this one simple practice, *Saminchakuy,* it is possible to develop our full human spiritual potential, if our practice is diligent and dedicated.

## NATURE CONTEMPLATION #1: *SAMINCHAKUY*

### Absorbing Finest Energy of the Cosmos and Offering Heavy Energy to Mother Earth.

Sit or stand in a quiet calm place where you won't be interrupted for at least ten minutes. (When you get good at this, you can do it in two minutes or even seconds!)

Bring your awareness to the beating of your heart, your breathing, and then to the flow of your own life force moving throughout your body. Now notice that the living energy that is you, fills your body and extends beyond your body, surrounding you like a Bubble. Since you are living energy and so is everything else, this means you can connect, communicate and collaborate with everything else via your personal energy Bubble. Since energy is moved by intention you must now lovingly activate your will – your *munay.*

Continue sitting or standing comfortably wherever you are. Use whatever image you like of our Cosmos. If you wish, imagine the star-studded night sky over the Big Island of Hawaii showing the great thick white band of our home galaxy, the Milky Way. Imagine the living Cosmos studded with billions and billions and stars and loads of galaxies. All of those stars and the Cosmos above our heads produce an infinite amount of finest energy. Perceive the Cosmos as living energy.

Now bring your awareness to the top part of your Bubble. Open the top of your Bubble just above your head and receive the influx of this finest living energy of the superabundant Cosmos, an influx of Cosmic Nectar. At this moment the finest living energy of the Cosmos is pouring in filling your entire Bubble and entering into all the cells of your body cleansing and invigorating and refreshing you with new life force. This is your birthright, just like breathing fresh air. Keep on drinking in this finest energy into your entire body, filling your head, throat, heart, lungs, belly, hips, legs, feet with fresh new energy. Fill your entire body and your entire Bubble with finest living energy of the Cosmos. Once you feel FULL of finest living energy throughout your body and your Bubble spend a moment to ENJOY THIS SENSATION.....Ahh.

Now take a moment to notice that you are standing on an enormous living being, that has gravity, Mother Earth. Bring your attention to the bottom of your Bubble surrounding your feet and the Earth. You may notice that your Bubble naturally extends down into *Pachamama* anywhere from a few inches to a foot or so. Using your *munay*, your loving intention, open the bottom of your Bubble and offer, along with love your, all the heavy energy that has been accumulating in your Bubble with nowhere to go.

Offer this heavy energy as a sacred gift (remember it is not bad-just heavy) along with your love to Mother Earth. Release this heavy energy with no more guilt or remorse than you have in exhaling, knowing that your heavy energy is a gift of food for other beings. *Hoocha* is the favorite food of Mother Earth, as she is the great composter of all things material and energetic.

You can feel the heavy energies flowing down your legs and out your feet into Mother Earth and your feet may even become heavy, tingly, or feel magnetized to the ground. You are using your intention to connect your energy field to Mother Earth and to release your heavy energy to her as a sacred gift. She knows exactly what to do with it, just like worms know what to do with the orange peel you put in your compost pile in the back yard. Your heavy energy to her is the same as that orange peel is to the worms.

Trust Mother Earth to know what she is doing and enjoy the outflow of these heavy energies that naturally and organically flow down your legs because they no longer belong in your Bubble. Keep releasing your heavy energy until the outflow starts to slow down and you feel a sense of relief.

If you are feeling better...bravo! If now, you notice that your head hurts or your tummy aches or that you now really feel that chronic pain in your back, bravo again. This means you have released the layers that keep you desensitized to your own physical experience. If you feel like crying, cry. Crying is another way to release heavy energy and also certain toxins that gather in your brain, and can only come out through tears.

Now return your attention back to the top of your Bubble and absorb finest energy from our infinite Cosmos, filling in all the places from which you just released your heavy energy. Refill your body and your Bubble with finest nectar of the Cosmos, especially bringing that energy into any areas of pain or tension in your body or into any areas of injury or hurt, be they physical, mental or emotional. ENJOY THIS!

This time when you release your heavy energy, release the heaviness from any area of chronic pain or tension in your body.

Release your anger and sadness; release your doubts, worries and fears and anxieties. Release any energies that belong to other people. Release, with much love to Mother Earth, everything that is ready to be released from your Bubble and offer it to her as a sacred gift, just as you offered your carbon dioxide to the plants and trees, with love and gratitude.

When you feel the flow of heavy energy subsiding, return your attention once again to the top of your Bubble and receive finest energy one last time, refilling your Bubble with cosmic nectar and refreshing your entire energy system. Open your Bubble at your feet and offer any remaining heavy energies to Mother Earth until you have created a wonderfully grounded and connected sense of well being in your body and your Bubble, and between you, the Earth and the Cosmos.

Congratulations! You have just practiced *Saminchakuy*.

Now take a moment to notice how you feel. Has your feeling state changed from when you first began this exercise ten minutes ago? If so, how? Do you feel lighter? Happier? Peaceful? More connected? Relieved? Free?

Simple…right? Make an intention to do this exercise every time you need it. Most of us would never go five or six days without taking a shower, would we? We need to make a new habit of cleaning our energy Bubble every day, just like we enjoy taking a shower everyday. We must care for our energy Bubble just as we care for our physical body. We call this "Bubble hygiene."

Jot down your own notes of your experience. Practice this exercise for five or ten minutes everyday for six weeks and track your experience. The result of the exercise is its own reward.

# NATURE CONTEMPLATION #2

## *SAYWAYCHAKUY*--Creating A Column of Living Energy

Now that we have received finest energy from the Cosmos and offered the yummy treat of our heavy energy to Mother Earth, the law of reciprocity provides us with another opportunity for exchange. Because we have offered to Mother Earth, we have a right to receive her finest living energy in return, and because we received from the Cosmos we must, by the law of *ayni*, return our finest living energy back to the Cosmos. This completes the great cycle of sacred energy exchange. Just as trees and plants take in our carbon dioxide (delicious for them) process and transform it back into life-giving oxygen for us (delicious for us) Mother Earth can receive all of our heavy energies (delicious for her) transform them into a life giving substance, her finest living energy (delicious and nutritious for us).

Bring your attention to your breathing, your heartbeat, and your own Bubble. Notice the living being of Mother Earth under your feet. Now open the bottom of your Bubble near your feet and simply receive the finest living energy or 'nectar' from Mother Earth knowing that because you gave to her, she will always give back to you by the sacred law of reciprocity. You now have a right to receive her finest energy. Draw finest Mother Earth Energy into your Bubble and fill your body and your Bubble. Now add your own personal finest living energy, your love and gratitude to that, and use all that delicious energy to build a beautiful lovely column of living energy that flows out of the top of your head up toward the Cosmos.

Continue to use your intention to pull finest energy from Mother Earth through your Bubble and add your finest energy to formulate a giant column of finest living energy flowing up into the heart of the Cosmos. Make sure your column of energy flows out of the top of your head and reaches all the way to the heart of the Cosmos to complete this cycle of reciprocity.

You have received finest energy from the Cosmos, offered your heavy energy to Mother Earth, received her finest energy in return and now offer back your finest energy to the Cosmos, one complete cycle. Congratulations! You have just completed one great cycle of energetic reciprocity between You, Earth, and Cosmos through something we all share, our field of living energy. Now just take a moment to notice how you feel. Has your perception shifted or changed in any way. How does your Bubble feel now? Do you have any new insights or sensations? Songs? Colors? Messages? Music? Take a moment to jot down or draw whatever comes to you

# CHAPTER THREE

# IT'S ALL GOOD

## Principle 3. *YANANTIN* :HARMONIOUS RELATIONSHIP BETWEEN COMPLEMENTS

*Yanantin* **philosophy is the celebration of difference. All differences are beneficial and complementary, male/female, hot/cold, night/day, heavy/fine. Living energy is neither positive nor negative, rather it is 'heavy' and 'fine.' All energy is useful. Collaborative exchange of differences is life-affirming.**

In the Andean worldview, there are no conflicting opposites, only harmonizing complements. It is a philosophy celebrating the sacredness of *difference*. Male and female, night and day, hot and cold, or heavy and fine energy are not opposites; they are complementary energies that provide a life-affirming whole. This philosophy can be encapsulated in the Quechua word *Yanantin*, which means "harmonious relationship between different or complementary things."

All living energy is useful. All energy is part of a system. In fact, as we discussed in the last chapter, complementary energies function together to create life, in a series of sacred exchanges.

When we really think about it, we realize that "good" and "bad" are simplistic labels that don't accurately define our world or its living energies. The Inkas do however differentiate energy by frequencies, some energy is heavier and some is more refined as you have seen in the language the Inkas use to categorize these different types of energies. Finest energies are described are called *sami (nectar)* and dense or heavy energy is called *hoocha*, and we human beings can definitely perceive the difference.

While releasing heavy energy or *hoocha* benefits human beings, this does not mean that *hoocha* is bad. *Hoocha* is not "bad" energy any more than a negatively charged particle is a "bad" particle. In fact, when *hoocha* is in the right place, it is very valuable energy. Think about how it feels to release *hoocha* to Mother Earth. The act of offering our *hoocha* to Mother Earth actually makes us feel very powerfully grounded, stabilized, and magnetically connected to Mother Earth, and this is of great benefit.

Fine energy (nectar) needs to be constantly ingested just as we need fresh oxygen, food and water; while heavy energy needs to be released, just as we must exhale, sweat, pee, and pooh in order to maintain health. Heavy and fine energies need to be moved or 'flowed' to the right place to produce their natural and beneficial effects. And it is up to us humans to do it, as we are the mobile units of Nature. Following the law of gravity, heavy naturally goes down.

If you have trouble thinking of heavy as good, just imagine there is suitcase of gold and a suitcase of feathers in front of you, and it's up to you to choose which one you want. Clearly the suitcase of feathers is much lighter than that heavy suitcase full of gold. Which suitcase do you want? Which is more useful to you?

Think of your heavy energy as gold -a powerful currency of exchange. Your heavy energy *is* gold for other beings, just as carbon dioxide is food for plants, and plants emit oxygen that is "gold" for us.

In the previous chapter I elaborated the Inka description of the Lower, Middle and Upper Worlds. Each of these worlds is differentiated by their living energies. The upper world (cosmos) or *hanaq pacha*, is a place filled with highly refined energies. The middle world, Kay Pacha, is a mix of fine and heavy energies, and the lower world is the location of heavier energies. Let me state again that the Lower World, *Ukhu Pacha*, is very different from the Western concept of "hell." *Ukhu Pacha* is a place of heavier energies inhabited by denser beings; however, it is not a bad place. It is just a place of more gravitational force –like the bottom of the ocean-- a heavier place. Just as the pressure of earth on coal produces diamonds, the *Ukhu Pacha* also produces treasures. We can harvest these treasures once we begin to apply the concept of complementary differences, rather than our simplistic 'good' and 'evil' framework.

I consider the concept of *Yanantin* to be the cure to our most basic Western philosophical misapprehension about life. *Yanantin* dismantles the very foundation we have been taught: to conceptualize everything in our lives as good and bad.

Think about it. Everywhere we go we have the good and bad categories drilled in to our heads. We speak casually of the "good" and "bad" restaurants and movies, the "good" and "bad" neighborhoods. However, we all know that life is more subtle. The "good" guys don't always wear white hats and the "bad" guys sometimes do good things.

The practice of polarizing everything into categories of opposites becomes ludicrous when you truly examine it. In Nature, do we observe good and bad animals and plants? Of course not, as each plays a specific role in the ecosystem Nature designed. A milk thistle in my pasture is not good for my sheep, but if I place it in my medicinal garden it becomes extremely useful. A poisonous tree frog in its jungle environment serves as a natural and important part of the ecosystem, but it's not useful at all in my salad. An opera singer working in a fast-food joint may make a downright "evil" hamburger, yet produce exquisite soul-relieving sound when placed on a stage. All energy is good and serves a beneficial purpose when it is in the right place.

I invite you to try living without good and bad categories for one day, one hour, or even for five minutes. During this time don't categorize in terms of good or bad, and see what happens.

A lovely Italian truck driver attended one the very first classes I taught in Milan. He was a huge man with soft eyes and an enormous mane of curly hair. When I suggested to the class to stop codifying life in terms of good and bad, he had an epiphany! He came back to my next class three months later, telling me that for seventeen years he had driven the same truck route, a route with its' distinctly "good towns" and "bad towns." Curiously enough, bad things always happened in the towns the truck driver thought of as "bad towns." He decided to make the experiment and stop thinking of them in this way. His face was alight, his eyes wide with astonishment with his big shaggy golden curls wagging, as he reported back to us that after seventeen years, he had only now discovered that "all the towns are good towns!"

When we think about ourselves as being filled with complements that harmonize, rather than as being composed of opposites that conflict, we are provided with an interesting opportunity to change our own behavior. We can view everything in our lives -every experience, person, place and situation - as an *opportunity to create a harmonious relationship through practicing reciprocal exchange.* This framework gives us more possibilities than our good and bad categories offer us.

The Inkas posited three stages of relationship they called *tinkuy (*encounter), *tupay* (conflict, challenge, competition) and *taqe* (joining or harmonizing). For those who engaged in the second stage, *tupay* or competition, the Inkas had a rule: the victor of a *tupay* was always obligated to teach his/her competitor how s/he won. This is a community-enhancing view as well as a highly productive use of competition. Imagine if our corporations operated by this principle!

As an organic farmer, I have never wished to be part of the "system," because ours is an artificial man-made system that is often more bio phobic than biophilic. However, I am a willing and devoted member of our *eco*system. Nature's great ingenious life-affirming playground offers me love, food, beauty, happiness, shelter, nectar, clothes, and a place to belong, to protect and care for. With the simple tools I have learned from the descendants of the Inkas, I can practice my devotion everyday. And in the concept of *Yanantin*, Inka wisdom offers a powerful tool for beneficial exchanges.

Leaders in the Inka Empire were expected be able to create *taqe* - to find the way to harmonize two different kinds of people, two different points of view, or two different fields of energy. Some historians now believe that the unparalleled expansion of the Inka Empire during the fifteenth century occurred largely through the leaders' ability to make *taqe* with the 150 or so diverse ethnic groups that made up the Inka Empire. The Inkas only considered war as a last resort, as it was more practical if these diverse ethnic groups *voluntarily* joined the Inka Empire, which many did.

Once they convinced another group of the benefits incurred by joining the Empire, the Sapa Inka (Sole Lord or High King) would literally exchange his fine vicuña wool clothing with the Chief or tribal leader of the new group and walk through the towns together to visually demonstrate that the two groups had now become one. This is a visual example of making *taqe* and a demonstration of the peaceful side of Inka Empire building.

If one takes the hint from Mother Earth and Father Sun— then we learn that there is a harmonious relationship possible between these two very different beings. Mother Earth is fertile, dark and receptive. Father Sun is hot, light, and dynamic. Together they create life. There is no war between Mother Earth and Father Sun! They are different yet harmonious. The Inkas believed these beings to be our greatest teachers. If we can personally, viscerally, emotionally, and psychologically identify with Nature and our planetary body to such an extent that we can feel ourselves to be what we in fact are; an integral part of her WHOLE, only then can we begin to have an idea of how to direct our human society.

With the outlook granted by *yanantin*, we are able to experience Male and Female qualities as life-affirming complements instead of opposites. The "war" between the sexes is over because we can retain our differences, yet be together. A great example of *yanantin* can be found in the metaphor of musical harmony. In order to sing harmony each individual must hold their own note, (maintain their difference) while listening to the other singer. The two notes together make a sound more pleasing than only one can make alone. This is the idea of a *yanantin* relationship in a human couple. The perfected form of the sacred couple is called "Hapu."

One of the best living examples of *yanantin* I can think of is a beautiful Q'ero couple named Don Humberto Sonqo and

Doña Bernardina Apaza. Their initiation story is a testament to the living practice of *yanantin* philosophy in Q'eros. Don Humberto Sonqo is from the Q'ero village of Charqapata and Doña Bernardina was born in Colpa Qucho, the Q'ero village at the foot of their sacred mountain, WAMANLIPA.

These two healers fell in love at the tender age of 14 and 15, each following in the footsteps of their parents and grandparents who were also healers. After working together for a year they both grew very ill and went to see the highest Q'ero Priest to look for a remedy. First the priest told them they were ill because they were working with their stars outside their bodies (more on this in chapter 6). Next, the priest said he would only give them the Initiation that would heal them if they promised ALWAYS to use the power he would give them to work together as a sacred healing couple to help others. Don Humberto had to promise to call the *Apus*, (mountain spirits, or most primary male forces of Nature) to help people together with Doña Bernardina. She likewise had to promise to use her powerful connection with Pachamama (the most primary female force of Nature) to work TOGETHER with Don Humberto to help and heal others. They made their solemn vow and received their initiation.

Now, more than fifty years later this couple are amongst the most popular healers from the Q'ero community and have been invited to travel the world several times over, sharing their healing expertise. As Don Humberto says, his trickster eyes glinting with mischief, "like it or not, I HAVE to work with her," while Doña Bernardina rolls her eyes, slugs him on the shoulder and agrees what a terrible trial it is, emitting her characteristic belly chuckle. They are a most lovely and devoted couple with five children and many grandchildren.

Once, while visiting my farm in Hawaii for a series of

teachings, this couple agreed to be interviewed by a man writing a book on couples who worked together in spiritual healing. He asked the normal Western question, "what do you do when you get irritated with each other and get into a conflict you can't resolve." I will never forget the look on their faces when the translator told them the question. They looked at him uncomprehendingly and responded, "Why would we do that when we have such a beautiful life together?"

One of the last living Fourth-Level priests of Q'eros attended the First World Conference on the Inka Tradition held in Grado, Italy next door to Venice, in May of 2003. A fervent Italian man asked, "What is the most important thing a man can achieve in his lifetime?" Don Mariano Apaza looked at him calmly and answered, "The biggest achievement a man can make in his lifetime is to understand his wife and make a good life with her." More than a few jaws dropped at his answer. However, this is the perfect response of a Fourth Level Priest because he is talking about the practical application of the Inka philosophy of *yanantin* to make his life better.

As an interesting aside, information gathered by Oscar Nunez del Prado from the first expedition to Q'ero shows a fascinating sexual ethic that was and still is an intrinsic part of Q'ero culture. From the age of sexual maturity all sexual relations were free and open until the time a couple decided they wanted to stay together. At that time the couple was required to find the highest priest of their village and ask for a coca leaf reading to see if their union was blessed in the *Kawsay Pacha*. If the energy world agreed then no one could stop the couple from getting married.

# INKA WEAVING

During the Inka Empire, the Q'ero were the royal weavers, tending the vicuñas that live at high altitude, with great love and respect to produce the finest wool for the Sapa Inka, Sapa Qoya and the rest of the Royal family. In fact, traditional Q'ero weavings are what inspired the first academic expedition to Q'eros in 1955. Q'ero villages had been *relatively* isolated from the rest of humanity making up part of a remote Spanish Hacienda since the conquest. When Anthropologist Oscar Nuñez del Prado saw the Q'ero at the Q'ollorit'i Festival, in 1949, he was astonished to recognize traditional Inka designs in their ceremonial clothing, designs that were thought to have been wiped out by the Spanish "extirpation of idolatry" in the 17th and 18th centuries. Further their proud bearing and the fact that they proclaimed, "we are Inkas," spurred him to begin research that resulted in the 1955 expedition.

Today the Q'ero still live at impossibly high altitude, in the seven villages now known as the Q'ero Nation, known as the "Last Inka Ayllu," where they continue to be the keepers of Alpaca and Vicuña. A vicuña is a small camelid, related to the Llama and Alpaca, that produces uniquely soft fur from its chest hairs, harvested only once every eighteen months.

For the Q'ero, weaving is both a physical and an energetic act, just as it was in the time of the Inka Empire. The entire process - from tending the animals with love, to spinning the wool, to creating the beautiful weavings – all this is implied in one Quechua word, *awaspa*. Weaving different energies together to create harmony and beauty is the practice of *Yananchakuy*.

Now that you have perceived the world as living energy, and have experienced the act of breathing as a sacred exchange with, and you have cleaned your bubble with *sami* and released your *hoocha* by practicing AYNI, sacred exchange, through *Saminchakuy* and *Saywachakuy, you* are ready to move onto the third Inka practice still used in Q'ero communities today. Its' Inka name is *yananchakuy,* and it is the practice of circulating complementary energies with a human partner. In this practice we create *taqe* on an energetic level. *Yananchakuy* literally translates as "getting married." It is also known as the practice of "melting bubbles."

For this exercise you will need to find a partner of the complementary sex, or if you prefer, find anyone who has a difference that complements your own qualities: you are tall, they are short, you are black, they are white, you are a lawyer, they are an artist, you are gay, they are straight, you are male, they are female, etc. In other words, you can do this with any other human being. DO try a number of combinations just for fun and experience.

After you have found your partner with whom you want to play, first practice *Saminchakuy* and *Saywachakuy* together, cleaning your bubbles before you begin. Now you are ready to circulate energy together.

# Nature Contemplation #3: YANANCHAKUY

# Melting Bubbles

Stand back to back with about one foot of distance between you. Next decide who prefers to move their energy earthward and who prefers to move their energy skyward. Traditionally, women have a natural connection to the earth, and men have a natural connection to the sky---but we all know that isn't always so. Just pick one and communicate with your partner so that you know who's going up and who's going down. For the simplicity of the description and to avoid confusion I am going to call the downward energy mover Partner 1 and the upward energy mover Partner 2. Partner 1, you are moving energy earthward. Place your right hand on the top of your own head and your left hand on your sacrum. Partner 2, you are moving energy skyward. Place your right hand on your tail and your left hand on the top of your head. The right hand is active and the left is receptive.

Partner 1, open the top of your bubble and receive finest energy of the cosmos into the top of your head. Using your intention and cosmic *sami*, send a pulse of energy from your right hand on the top of your head down through your brain and spine into your tail to connect to your left hand.

Partner 2, open the bottom of your bubble and pull up finest energy from Mother Earth. Then use it to send a pulse of energy from your right hand on your tail up your spine to the top of your head to connect with your left hand. Once you both feel that your right and left hands are connected by a stream of energy running either up or down your spine, then let your hands fall naturally to your sides and place yourselves back to back, so that you are touching bodies yet still standing on your own feet. Don't lean against each other - maintain your weight on your own two feet.

Partner 1, you will continue to pull energy down your spine, into your tail and then offer it to Mother Earth. Now pull Mother Earth energy up into your tail. Then put together your sami with Mother Earth sami and send it from your tail into the tail of your partner. Send all that delicious *sami* out from your tail and into your partners tail. Focus and use your *Munay*.

Partner 2, you will pull the energy from your partners tail into your tail, and pull it up your spine, offering it from the top of your head to the cosmos. Now receive finest energy of the cosmos and put that together with your love, your *sami*. Now send all that nectar cascading down into the top of your partner's head.

Partner 1, continue to pull the energy from the top of #2's head and pull it back down your spine and receive finest energy of Mother Earth. Put it together with your love and send all that Sami out your tail and into your partners' tail.

Together you are forming an energy ring of power that circulates in one direction, connecting both of you in one energy Bubble. This may not happen right away and may take some time using your focus and concentration to really get the energy circuit going. Take your time and keep focusing until you feel the ring of energy is moving. Use your intention, your *munay*, to continue this energy circulation and keep it going for at least 4 or 5 minutes until you feel the energy has harmonized between you, making the two of you into one larger energy bubble.

This exercise should be done in silence giving priority to your personal experiences of the movement of energies.

Allow your bodies to move and sway if they wish to. Do maintain your weight on your own two feet while you "circulate your differences" together. Make sure you keep at it long enough to experience the development of a sense of harmony together.

If it continues to feel uncomfortable, try circulating the other way. In other words, change the direction of the flow: the person who was moving energy downward before, now moves it upward and vice versa. Usually every couple has one way that will feel easier or more 'natural' but either way will work.

When you feel it is complete, finish the exercise by stepping apart, separating bodies and bubbles and turn to face your partner. Thank each other for the exchange in any way you wish. Then verbally share your experience. You may wish to notate your experiences. We recommend you first try this exercise with partners with whom you feel a very good and comfortable relationship. You will notice that in every Inka exercise we always RECEIVE *SAMI* FIRST, then release *hoocha*, as this is the most organic and natural way for your bubble to clean itself. Were you to release all your heavy energy first, you could collapse.

Just like running water, this exercise offers a way for each person to help clean the bubble of the other by circulating *sami* through each others bubbles, connecting to the delicious *sami* sources of Father Cosmos and Mother Earth.

On to Principle 4!

# CHAPTER FOUR

# INKA SEED: SACRED CENTER

## Principle 4. INKA MUJU (ENERGY SEED): QOSQO/SACRED CENTER

**Everything from to cells to animals to human bodies to cities to planets to Galaxies have a central digestive system—that is both physical and energetic. We humans can activate the power of our sacred center to create health and well-being in ourselves, families, cities, nations. Within our sacred center lies our Inka Seed that holds the seven levels of our complete human potential.**

The Andean Masters say that every human on earth has the capacity to grow to the seventh level of spiritual development because each of us holds within us our Inka Seed. The Inka Seed contains the energetic potential of each human beings' unique and complete spiritual unfoldment, and no two seeds are the same.

It is, of course, only fitting that the Andean Masters define human spiritual development in Natural terms. The concept of the Inka Seed is a grand Nature metaphor, but it is so much more than that. It is an explanation of the process of human energetic growth. We literally hold within us a core bundle of energy. This core bundle, the Inka Seed, grows just like an ordinary seed grows –the earth must be warmed and ter must soften the outer casing, in order to cause germination.

Once germinated, the small plant has to feed itself by creating sacred exchanges with the forces of Nature: Water, Earth, Sun, Wind and Cosmos. Our Inka seed is planted deep within the warm 'earth' of our sacred center, and lies dormant, safe within its hard outer casing, waiting for the right triggers or cues from the environment signaling that it is time to begin to grow.

This spiritual growth refers to the literal expansion our energy Bubbles so that we are able to incorporate and resonate with ever-larger systems of Nature. With correct feeding we are able to grow our Bubbles, i.e., enlarge our resonant field. To begin we must first warm the earthy center that is our QOSQO or spiritual stomach...awakening our Inka Seed. Our Inka Seed defines us as sacred beings of limitless energetic capacity, inherently connected to the greater forces of Nature that are alive—like, for example, mountains.

Many Western people who live at the foot of a mountain may confess they feel a sense of 'protection' from the mountain. Just for a minute let's consider this from a purely practical point of view. Mountains gather clouds, providing rain for crops, and actually protect us from winds and harsher weather. Here is a quote from weatherman Josh Fitzpatrick:

> *"In essence the Appalachian Wedge acts like a bubble, protecting us from major ice and snowfalls. Also a southeast or east wind off the mountains is a warmer and drier wind and this too protects many of us."*

Interesting choice of the word 'bubble," Josh! This could almost make my Inka friends think you are beginning to understand.

My farm in Hawaii is nestled into one of the folds of the beautiful and magnificent Mauna Loa—the largest mountain in the world. I have lived here through at least five hurricanes predicted to cause major devastation that ended up doing little to none, and actually provided some great surf. Many consider it to be the sheer mass of Mauna Loa Mountain that protects us from hurricanes.

Clearly it is often logical and practical to consider mountains as protectors. The difference between our point of view and the *Inka* point of view is that they NEVER forget to be grateful for this, and for them the Mountain is alive with its' own spirit, its' own form of consciousness. The Inkas have a name for the living consciousness of a Mountain; they call it an *Apu*, pronounced **ahh-poo**. *Apu* actually means 'spirit' or 'lord' and is a title of great respect and honor. To comprehend their framework of spiritual development one must know who the *Apus* are.

Even more than protectors the *Apus* are literally Nature beings that have domain over the people, plants, and animals of the area they supervise. The Inkas have a highly formulated and detailed hierarchy of Mountains Spirits complete with names and clearly defined personalities. The *Apus* not only contain a specific type of living energy that is needed by people, they are also very willing to share it. For example if you are a very serious person your family will send you on a pilgrimage to the Mama Simona, one of the rare female *Apus* known to be a real partier, so that you can receive her power of enthusiastic play.

On the other hand, if you have a rather weak personality, you may be sent on a pilgrimage to *Apu Ausangate* who is known for his power of authority, so that you can gain a more commanding personality. The *Apus* are powerful beings and initiates seek to integrate their power.

Now I will outline the seven levels of Inka psychospiritual development, beginning with a diagram of the first four levels, that have to do with the *Apus,* the ancient Inka system of governance, and our human ability to resonate with and thereby literally communicate, with Nature.

# THE FOURTH LEVEL

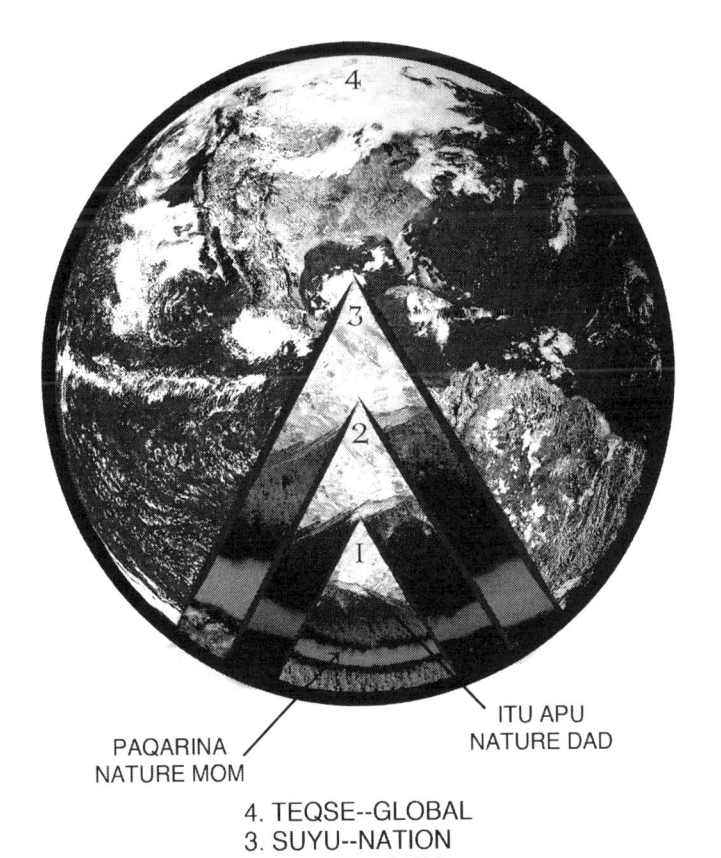

PAQARINA
NATURE MOM

ITU APU
NATURE DAD

4. TEQSE--GLOBAL
3. SUYU--NATION
2. LLAQTA--CITY
1. AYLLU- VILLAGE

IMAGE 1

# THE SEVEN LEVELS OF PSYCHOSPIRITUAL DEVELOPMENT

## Level 1—*AYLLU*

*AYLLU* means family in Quechua. *Apu* means 'lord' or spirit that inhabits the peaks of Mountains. It is literally the consciousness of the Mountain. From an energetic point of view this level is defined by our ability to resonate our Bubble with our human family and with our village or small town, including our local mountain spirit. The *Ayllu Apus* protect and oversee the welfare of a family or small village. Someone who is able to resonate their bubble with the *Ayllu Apus* can effectively communicate with them, and could potentially govern a small village.

## Level 2—*LLAQTA*

*LLAQTA* means city. The second level is defined by our ability to resonate our Bubble with a larger human group within the larger geographic area of a city, and the accompanying larger Nature beings. The *Llaqta Apus* oversee cities, or a group of villages. From the point of view of an Andean Priest this energetic resonance means we are able to speak to the *Llaqta Apus*. If we can communicate with the lords of a city we are thereby potentially capable to govern or be a true leader of that area.

## Level 3—*SUYU*

*SUYU* means region. The Inka Empire was called *Tawantinsuyu* which means the 'four regions together.' The third level is defined by our ability to identify, and thus resonate our Bubble, with a region or Nation - meaning the people, the geography, and the Nature Beings. A Nation is a group of cities including humans and Nature beings. The Nature Beings responsible to oversee the welfare of an entire Nation are called *Suyu Apus*. A person at the third level of human development is able to communicate with the *Suyu Apus* and thus potentially govern a region.

To our Western thinking, a person who can resonate their Bubble with the Nature Beings of a Nation would be quite unusual and advanced. Such a person would be something like a King or Queen of old. A good example is seen in the ancient Celtic ritual in which the King must literally marry with the land. For the Inka, one who can speak with the Lords or Apus of a Nation or group of cities is one who could have the capacity to govern that area. However, in the Inka framework, the third is the level of the adolescent.

Further confirmation of this system came one afternoon as we were chatting with a Q'ero paqo named Don Francisco Apaza. When we asked him to tell us more about the levels of Paqos he came out with something astonishing. He spoke of the governors of different areas using the 16th century terms "Qoyana, Payan, Cayao" which reference directly to the Suyu, Llaqta, and Ayllu levels. The fact that a modern Q'ero still possesses knowledge of terms of the governance system of the 16th century shows the faithfulness of the Q'ero oral tradition. It is only upon advancing to Level 4 that one becomes an adult on this earth, or Kurak Akulleq—literally meaning "most experienced chewer of coca leaves."

To help us understand this system let's take an example from Nature once again. How about a hive of bees? Each day the worker bees go out to gather nectar and pollen from the flowers of a specific area, usually about a four-mile radius from the hive. They bring nectar back and feed it to the QUEEN who receives that nectar, a kind of information of the area. The Queen then lays eggs for the hive, producing up to her own body weight in eggs everyday. With the nectar she receives she exudes pheromones that regulate the harmony of the entire hive, usually 30 to 60 thousand inhabitants. She is truly the governor of her hive!

## Level 4—*TEQSE*

*TEQSE* means global. The *Teqse Apus* are the Nature Beings to whom everyone on earth has equal access. Each one of us on earth can see the sun, feel the wind on our faces, perceive the solidity of earth beneath us, listen to the music of running water, and stare in awe at the blaze of constellations in the night sky. These are the *Teqse Apus,* the living consciousness of each of these aspects or forces of Nature. They each provide a unique *Sami,* spiritual nectar, required for our human growth and evolution. The *Teqse Apus* are in charge of the well-being of all humans, animals, plants, insects, every creature on earth. They are our principal teachers. At the fourth level, they are the sources of our power and the ones we look to for guidance.

When we develop the capacity to resonate our energy Bubble with the entire electromagnetic field of Mother Earth we are considered to have achieved the fourth level—the Inka definition of adulthood. To achieve the *fullness* of the fourth level one must apply one's *munay* to continue to evolve.

According to the Andean Masters, there are no humans walking the earth today who have achieved the Fifth, Sixth or Seventh levels. But Inka history says the fifth and sixth levels have been manifest as recently as the 16th century, less than five hundred years ago! Our knowledge of the levels beyond the fourth, comes only through descriptions orally transmitted by Fourth Level priests Don Benito Qoriwaman and Don Andres Espinoza, to their faithful students. No Andean Master ever spoke directly of the resonant energy fields that correlate with the next three levels, but logical extension of the metaphor implies this, and fits quite neatly and 'naturally' into the Seven Level framework.

## Level 5—*INKA MALLKU, ÑUST'A*

Fifth Level initiates are those who can resonate their Bubble with the living energy of our entire Solar System. Individuals of this level are said to have walked the earth during the Inka Empire, and are prophesied to return. A male initiate is called Inka Mallku and a female initiate is called Ñust'a. They will be known by their capacity to heal every illness, every time, with only one touch.

## Level 6—*SAPA INKA, SAPA QOYA*

Sixth Level initiates are those who can resonate their personal Bubble with the entire energy field of our Milky Way Galaxy. They are considered to be truly enlightened spiritual leaders. The Inka High King and High Queen (Sapa Inka and Sapa Qoya) were known to be sixth level initiates who possessed the power to glow with their own light.

Level 7—*TAYTANCHIS RANTI* means equivalent of God on Earth. A human of the seventh level would be able to resurrect their physical body from death and possess the ability to resonate their personal energy Bubble with the entire universe.

The Andean Masters say that the majority of humanity has more or less made it to the third level. Most of us have developed a National identity of some kind. We relate with our human language group. To resonate with a Nation is quite an achievement that must not be undervalued. Still, we cannot remain here indefinitely – just as we can't remain in adolescence indefinitely but must continue our growth towards adulthood.

Just as in adolescence, the key attribute of the third level is *conflict*. Imagine the task of adolescence but at the National level. We are fighting to establish our identity as any good adolescent must do. We are trying to find out who we are and how powerful we are, and we want to feel our boundaries and push our edges. We are flopping around trying to find our own inner authority and autonomy, and the way to do this is through conflict -War.

Nowhere is the adolescent mind more clearly visible than in the theater of War. War is an immature overreaction to a perceived threat. It springs from a disempowered state of fear, and derives from a lack of impulse control. One can clearly see that the concept of War as an engine of economic growth comes again from the adolescent mind, providing short-term benefits to the very few, and great harm to many, whereas the mature adult sees that War is not a sustainable solution to long-term problems.

To have an adolescent mentality is a natural stage in the growth cycle. One cannot bypass adolescence. Yet neither can an individual or a society remain forever at this undeveloped stage. Sadly so far, our society has been producing relatively few adults.

Were we to have a society of true adults we would become responsible, self-organizing, and naturally tolerant of diversity. In a simplified description of the adolescent state of awareness, authority is still found outside the self. We require manmade laws and police to enforce our adherence to rules. FEAR is the primary emotion, and the principal mind state is one of the victim/perpetrator that characterizes ones' relationships at this level of development. One seeks self through conflict and projection of the shadow. We are constantly moving through the victim/ perpetrator cycle, and the powerless /power-over game. In our political and corporate systems this has become a normative behavior known as "swimming with sharks." My apologies to the sharks! This sadly adolescent power game is regaled, and held up to be the "necessary behavior of the successful person." It has nothing to do with integrity, goodness, altruism, sincerity, authenticity or honor. It is not the behavior of what my husband's grandmother would call "grown folks."

All is catalyzed by fear and fight or flight, kill or be killed, eat or be eaten. From this lens of perception there is only one true religion and "it's mine!" All other religions must therefore be untrue and must be destroyed because they are a threat. At this level of our development we are continuously (consciously or unconsciously) seeking to conflict in order to learn and know about who we are. We are attempting to exercise what we conceive to be our personal power.

All these behaviors lead to the production of the seven heavy energies of the unconscious, which reach a peak at the third level. These energies are generated through the emotional states of FEAR, GREED, JEALOUSY, SHAME, ANGER/HATRED, ARROGANCE and DECEIT. If one believes Netflix series like "House of Cards" to be true, the willingness to swim in the above energies is what now qualifies you for a job in Washington D.C.

The Seven energies of the unconscious kind of looks like a new list of the seven deadly sins, doesn't it? However, in the Inka tradition these are considered nothing more than the forms of heavy energy we produce in abundance during this adolescent period. Since we are trying to learn about them and see them, we project these qualities onto others to get a better view and then react to them. The state of inner anxiety and war becomes our normal. Jealousy, Greed, and Deceit run our world and become accepted behavior. All of this MUST be seen and known MUST be experienced or we can never get through to the next level. These heavy energies must be seen, touched, recognized and then put in order by the higher consciousness of the fourth level. All of this is very engaging and fascinating like a good soap opera. However, just like a good parent, it is the job of the fourth-level initiates to take responsibility and clean it up.

## THE FOURTH LEVEL

The Fourth Level solution is oh elegant. So simple. JUST EAT AND DIGEST YOUR OWN HEAVY ENERGY and...don't produce any more. Simple – yes; easy...NO! But don't worry, there is training, and we do have models—people living now who exemplify the fullness of the fourth level.

His Holiness the Dalai Lama is constantly telling us that the Chinese are our brothers and sisters. Never does he waiver from his understanding because he is able to maintain a larger viewpoint. While H.H. the Dalai Lama undoubtedly feels the pain and suffering of his people he demonstrates an extraordinarily mature level of impulse control. He provides us one of the few examples of true adult behavior. You may know individuals you already look up to who operate on the fourth level. They are sincere, altruistic, kind and truly generous people dedicated to helping others in real ways. Let me define a bit more the fourth level and then we can talk about how the Inka practices presented here directly address the key transition from third level to fourth.

At the Fourth level our primary emotions are LOVE & TRUST. Trust is essential in order to be able to move living energy. For love and trust, sincerity and honesty is required, nobility and selflessness. The Fourth Level human is dedicated to (and good at) creating harmony out of conflict. Our spiritual authority is located inside of ourselves, we are responsible for our lives, actions, and behaviors, and we accept and integrate the shadow aspects of ourselves without projecting them onto others.

We are in the 'drivers seat' of our lives and have a measured understanding of our importance in relationship to the whole. We are people of great generosity, honesty, sincerity, integrity, warmth, humility and empathy, but probably not all the time. We are not perfect and we know it and we accept others and their imperfections including those of the third level.

At the fourth level a whole host of societal ills find their resolution. If we can experience the pure 'masculine' power of our Father Sun, and the pure 'feminine' power of our Mother Earth, and we look to them as our guides for how male and female must interact, then there is no more war between the sexes.

At the fourth level we are focused on the living energy behind all manifested forms, so that the outer trappings and forms of religion (the stuff we fight about) become secondary and relatively unimportant. We begin to see that we can have the same encounter with the divine whether we are praying in a Catholic Church or meditating in a Buddhist temple or reciting a Jewish Prayer. The living energy of a prayer is fine energy, human nectar, whether it is Jewish, Buddhist, Christian, Hawaiian, Muslim, or Inka. Because perception is focused on the living energy behind outer forms, rather than the forms themselves—at the perspective of the fourth level, religious wars are over…done—solved.

This is part of the reason why the Andean people and ALL the Q'ero have no problem considering themselves devout Catholics AND Andean Priests of Nature, at the same time and without any contradiction. This is the reason why inside the Catholic Church on the main square of the *Plaza de Armas* in the central square of Cuzco there is a stone "Egg" from the principal altar of the Inkas at the front door opposite the Icon of the Virgin

Mary. This is why the Catholic Priests can go on with their Mass while the Andean Priests carry on their rituals with the egg at the same time and under the same roof. This is also why the Roman Catholic Arch Bishop of Cuzco can come to attend the Q'ollorit'i Festival and lead thousands of pilgrims in singing *Apuyaya Jesu Cristo*—O most powerful Mountain Spirit Jesus Christ. The Andean people are showing us the way to perceive the sacred energy of religion directly, beyond its outer forms and they are doing it with their hearts.

If our relationship with Nature is personal rather than a strange kind of disembodied schizophrenia, in which Nature is an object put here for our USE and/or ABUSE, then we will feel a moral imperative to care for her properly. In fact we are only caring for a larger extension of ourselves, one much needed for our continued survival. We then become independent, capable, responsible, self-directed empathic individuals working together in a great garden of humanity. This is indeed a much more practical and ultimately self-serving perspective. It is essential that we pass through a stage of development in which we can feel the body of Nature as our own body and identify with her completely as US. In this way only do we know how to guide our actions in scientific research, business, economics, and self-governance. How can we truly move into the future without the perspective of the whole planetary well-being as our guiding factor?

The beauty and peace of Nature, the necessity of oxygen - these are things we share as human beings; these things bind us together. The perspective of astronaut Edgar Mitchell, looking at the Earth from outer space and seeing the whole Earth as one being with all of us aboard - that is truly the point of view of the 4th level. This transformative perspective allows new solutions -- solutions that are not possible at the previous levels. This tradition calls upon us to be true scientists, to test our hypotheses against reality and see if they hold. I consider the following quote to be Einstein's description of the Fourth Level.

*"...There is a state of religious experience...that I will call cosmic religious feeling...there is no anthropomorphic conception of God corresponding to it. The individual feels the nothingness of human desires and aims and the sublimity and marvelous order which reveal themselves in Nature...I maintain that cosmic religious feeling is the strongest and noblest incitement to scientific research."*

--Albert Einstein

So traveling back from the grand vision of what a Fourth-Level society could be, to our present existence in everyday life...how does one begin the process of evolving to the fourth level?

We must now activate the mighty power of our *QOSQO*—our spiritual stomach. This pivotal practice is called *HOOCHA MIKHUY* (pronounced hoo-cha meek-whee).

Those of you who have been to Machu Picchu have no doubt traveled through the city of Cuzco, Peru. This ancient Inka capital is the oldest continuously inhabited city in the Western Hemisphere. Many don't know that the name Cuzco is a modern adaptation of the city's ancient Inka name – *Qosqo*, meaning navel of the Earth.

Inkas both ancient and modern still consider Cuzco/*Qosqo* as their Imperial city, sacred center, and "navel of the earth." In ancient times the central temple of *Qosqo*, known as the *Qorikancha*, contained the "Navel of the navel." This temple was used to eat and digest the heavy energy of the sacred city and in fact the entire Inka Empire.

If you spend time in Cuzco, you can still see that the entire city was designed in the form of a puma, with seven energy centers in the puma's body, paralleling the seven human energy centers that we will discuss in chapter five. According to my Quechua speaking friends that live in Cuzco, modern Cuzqueñans still say to each other, "Let's meet at the Puma's heart," or "see you at the Puma's throat at five o'clock."

As usual in Inka culture, everything 'mundane' from everyday life is also sacred, just as everything material also has an energetic aspect. So, in effect, nothing is ever really mundane.

The Inka, geniuses at recognizing and imitating natural structures, observed that the human physical body possesses the same energetic structure as the body of Mother Earth as a whole. The Earth, too, has a spiritual center. Like our own sacred center or belly, this area has the power to eat and digest heavy energy.

Nearly every culture in every continent in the world has a sacred place they call the "navel of the earth." I have personally visited the "omphalos" of the ancient Greeks as well as the one found in Rome. For the Hindu, Muslim, Chinese, Japanese, Hawaiian and every Native American Culture of North, Central, and South America, this idea of a sacred center seems 'central' to their spiritual tradition. From Cuzco to India to Rome to Jerusalem to Turkey to Borneo you can find a place considered by the Natives to be the "navel of the Earth." Clearly this concept has great meaning in our collective human consciousness. The importance of a sacred center that gathers, digests, and transforms is prevalent in our physiology as well as our psychology, and all of the world religions.

The sacred center, or a center that eats and digests, is a form that we see repeated everywhere in Nature. We humans have a central digestive system, and so do cells, plants, echinoderms, insects, and animals, and so do the cities of our Inka brothers and sisters, the Earth, and even our solar system. The Q'ero villages are designed around a sacred ceremonial center called Hatun Q'eros. In the Ka'u district of the Big Island of Hawai'i, just a few miles from my farm, lies the center of the district marked by a sacred Mountain called *Maka Na'au* which means roughly 'belly eye.' Once you start to investigate it's amazing just how pervasive this form appears, repeating itself throughout Nature from the microcosm to the macrocosm.

Astronomer Andrea Ghez, (pronounced 'gaze'--good name for an astronomer!) has done extensive research using KECK telescopes on Mauna Kea coupled with Scopes in Arizona and Chile, to provide us evidence that at the center of our galaxy lies a super massive black hole--an unimaginable force of suction--that draws everything into it and from which nothing escapes including light. Astronomers now postulate that this may be the natural structure of spiral galaxies in general and perhaps of most galaxies in the universe.

Everything in our universe eats and emits, and this is a life affirming process of all larger systems as well. There is now further evidence to suggest that perhaps black holes eat light and poop stars...or at least accrete a kind of matter that aids in the formation of stars. Just another one of those reciprocal exchanges brought to you by great Nature! The Inkas tell us that our energetic belly center has the exact same capacity and performs the same function, but on a human scale, as a black hole.

## WARMING YOUR INKA SEED

To wake up our Inka seed we must activate and learn to use our sacred center, our spiritual stomach or Qosqo, our human-sized black hole, collaborating with Mother Nature to put order in the energy world. Heavy and fine energies must be moved to their right places to create health and well being not only in ourselves, but also in our families, our homes, cities, and Nations.

We activate our Inka Seed by consciously learning how to operate our Qosqo. The Inkas say we have a physical stomach to eat and digest food, while our spiritual stomach "Qosqo" has the ability to eat and digest living energies. In this way we can help stimulate healing by digesting heavy energies from our own Bubbles, bodies, or from people or places where heavy energy may have collected or become stuck.

We humans are the only creatures that create *hoocha*, because we possess the gift of free will and can apply our will without love as well as intending harm to others. We can take without giving back (in facts it's the pirates code!). We can stop the natural flows of energy. These acts that go against the laws and flows of Nature create *hoocha*, and it is up to us to unstick, unblock and reopen the flows to bring *sami* where it is needed and eat *hoocha* wherever it is found. Therefore, the central healing practice of the Andean Priest (Paqo) is dedicated to helping our fellow humans by consciously activating the absorptive and digestive power of our spiritual stomachs to clean the *hoochas* we humans have created. In this way we can properly eat and digest 'heavy energies,' of people, places, and especially children, and animals, to encourage the flow of fresh fine energy to restore the systems of natural health.

Eating *hoocha* is the most fundamental function and responsibility of the Andean Priest. When we eat *hoocha*, we begin to warm and nourish the earthy center of our *Qosqo*, making a fertile ground in which our Inka Seed may activate. By helping our brothers and sisters we order the energy world, we help Mother Nature and move along on our path of spiritual development. Like all things designed by Nature, activating our *qosqo* provides mutual benefit to both ourselves and others. Just as it is natural for us to digest food, it is also natural for our spiritual stomach to digest heavy energies. Problems only arise when we are performing this natural function unconsciously or incompletely, or we are blocked by fear.

The spiritual stomach is activated on behalf of our fellow humans to help take away disease, as illness is said to follow from a lack of proper circulation of energies or an accumulation of heavy energy--a condition the Chinese call 'stagnant chi.' Heavy energy is very similar to the concept of stagnant chi. However, in our tradition, since we consider the heavy energy to be like gold, we actually seek to absorb it into our Belly eye in order to become more powerful. When we learn to become conscious heavy energy eaters, we help others without hurting ourselves. The ultimate heavy energy eater for us is MOTHER EARTH!

By now you have no doubt personally experienced that you can create a more healthy, happy and harmonious **YOU** by exchanging energies with Nature. Through the practice of eating heavy energy you can make more harmonious interactions with others, both human and non-human. Once you try these Inka practices, there is no going back, because the result of the practice is its own reward. The trick is to remember to use them when you need them, because once you release your heavy energy you can feel so much better that you actually forget you ever felt bad. That is why I encourage a daily practice. I feel so much joy from using this knowledge that the ONLY thing to do is share it with you.

The very act of inviting heavy energy *into* our bodies is one that some find to be counter intuitive due to the manner in which we inaccurately codify energies into 'positive' and 'negative.' I suggest that it is a true path to transformation since it offers a third solution of 'incorporation" that is based in a stance of personal power, not fear. Eating heavy energy requires an enormous alteration of our worldview. In order to be comfortable eating and digesting all kinds of energies, one can certainly no longer engage in the "positive" versus "negative" energy philosophy that is so prevalent in the current spiritual thinking. To be capable of eating *hoocha* one has to overcome one's fear.

In 2001 we had a student from Spain who attended the Hatun Qarpay ritual in Peru and decided to become AYNI MASTER. Upon returning home, she decided that wherever she went during her day she would begin each interaction at the bank, bakery or grocery store, by offering each person she encountered the nectar from her Bubble and eating their *hoocha* in exchange. She was a social worker so she had many daily interactions with many kinds of people. Shortly, in only several months, she was promoted to a position of much greater responsibility, overseeing nearly three hundred social workers. Clearly she was having more success, but even more importantly, she reported that she was having much more fun at her job!

You will notice that before attempting this practice we have prepared our Bubble in five ways. First we engaged in two preparatory exercises.

1) We practiced awareness of our Bubble by sensing everything as living energy.

2) We cleaned our Bubbles by consciously exchanging oxygen and finest energy with plants and trees.

Next we cleaned and empowered our Bubbles using the first three Inka Practices:

1) *Saminchakuy*: Receiving finest energy of the Cosmos and releasing our heavy energy to Mother Earth

2) *Saywachakuy*: Receiving finest energy from Mother Earth and returning our finest energy back to the Cosmos

3) *Yanachakuy*: Circulating finest energy of Earth and Cosmos with a partner.

We have prepared our point of view as well as our Bubble, quite thoroughly before attempting to eat the heavy energy of another person. Since this next Nature Contemplation involves a human partner, I suggest the two of you practice Contemplations 1-3 together before attempting this next key exercise.

## NATURE CONTEMPLATION #4: Hoocha Mikwhee

### To Eat and Digest Heavy Energy

Up until now we have received only finest energies from Nature Beings and released our own heavy energy. This is the first practice in which we will intentionally ingest heavy energy, which we will then **DIGEST**. By digesting heavy energy, we become more powerful, more grounded and connected to Mother Earth.

We are going to take it slowly and carefully and perform our first *Hoocha Mikwhee* in FOUR distinct steps.

1) Locate your belly eye

2) Practice opening and closing your Belly Eye

3) Eat and Digest your own heavy energy and finally

4) Eat and DIGEST the heavy energy of another person.

In order to practice eating heavy energy you must first locate your Qosqo---your spiritual stomach. In each person the precise location is slightly different, but generally within an inch or so of your belly button, matching more with the location of your physical stomach rather than your intestines.

## 1) LOCATE YOUR BELLY EYE

To locate your Qosqo, close your eyes and drop your awareness down inside your body to your belly area. Imagine that you are going to perceive or look out at the world through the eye of your belly. The late great Jimi Hendrix said it well in his famous song, "*Looking out my belly button window.*"

Now that your intention is in your belly, place your hand a few inches out in front of your belly and perceive the living energy of your hand through your belly eye. Use your total sense perception including visual, kinesthetic, intuitive…all your methods of knowing. Move your hand up and down in front of your belly to feel the point where you perceive the strongest contact between your belly and your hand. Then place your hand directly on that spot. Congratulations, you have just found your *Qosqo.*

## 2) PRACTICE OPENING & CLOSING YOUR BELLY EYE

Everything in Nature opens and closes. Imagine if you walked around with your mouth open all day! Even Black Holes have active and inactive periods. Now that you have located your belly eye you can begin the practice of consciously exercising it by intentionally opening and closing this central 'eye' of your Bubble.

Place your hand a few inches in front of your belly eye and as you move your hand further out in front of your belly, away from your body, imagine your belly eye opening wider like the lens of a camera until you feel your belly eye is wide open. Your hand may be anywhere from 6 to 24 inches out in front of you.

Now slowly bring your hand back toward your body while intending your belly eyes to close more and more as your hand gets closer to your body. Once your hand touches your body, your belly eye is fully closed.

Repeat opening and closing your belly eye by moving your hand away to open and bringing it back to touch your body to close your belly eye. Now with your regular eyes closed, once again open your belly eye and ask yourself.... "How do I feel with my belly eye open?"

What do you perceive? Are you comfortable? Uncomfortable?

Now bring your hand back and place it on top of your belly completely closing your belly eye . Notice: how do you feel now? Has your perception changed? If so, how? Are you more comfortable with your belly eye open or closed?

Here we are working (or playing) to activate and improve the natural functioning of our belly eyes. Due to our life experiences we may have belly eyes that are chronically stuck open or closed, so we are working to loosen any energy habits that impair natural opening and closing. So bear with it. Changing an energy habit can feel uncomfortable at first.

Those of us with chronically open Belly Eyes often feel overwhelmed by the emotional states of others. We feel compelled to take on their struggles or issues. Those of us with chronically closed belly-eyes often feel like observers sitting on the bleachers of our lives. We find it difficult to connect with others, feel a part of our world, or feel that we have any impact.

To work intentionally with your own *Qosqo* is to place yourself in the empowered center of your own life, literally and figuratively. Whatever may be the chronic state of your Qosqo, the great news is that all that can change with a little practice.

## 3) EAT & DIGEST YOUR OWN HEAVY ENERGY

Now to activate the capacity of your belly-eye! Drop your awareness down inside your body, place your hand on top of your belly-eye and open your belly eye. Now using your intention—your *munay*—pull all of the heavy energy FROM YOUR OWN BUBBLE ONLY into the center of your Belly Eye. If you have a headache or stomach ache, or any area of pain or tension in your body, concentrate especially to use the power of your '*Qosqo*' to pull the heavy energy from that area.

Notice how your Belly Eye is feeling as you continue to 'eat.' Are you getting full? Can you eat a little more? When you feel full...stop eating. Close your Belly Eye by bringing your hand back toward your belly and feel it close fully once your hand touches your belly.

Now command your spiritual stomach to DIGEST. You can feel the heavy energies flowing down your legs and into Mother Earth. You may feel some finer energies flowing up into your chest and head, or you may not—generally this sensation is much more subtle. This separation of the energies IS digestion. Your spiritual stomach works in just the same manner as does your physical stomach. Your digestive juices turn food into energy and you eliminate your waste. Just as you would never eat your food without noticing when you are full and without eliminating your waste, you must not eat living energy without DIGESTING! It is essential that the heavy energies flow naturally down your legs and out into Mother Earth. You may open the top of your Bubble to bring in finest energy of the cosmos to help encourage the flow of heavy energy down and out your feet.

If AND ONLY IF you feel GOOD, and that your belly-eye is now light and clean and free and your feet feel POWERFULLY magnetized to the earth…may you proceed to the next step. If not, you must find a nice place on the earth, (hopefully a green meadow or even just in your own bed at home) open your Belly Eye and lie face down on Mother Earth. Send your big root or *umbilical cord* down deep into Pachamama and offer her ALL the heavy energy from your Belly Eye. Once you feel the relief that Mother Earth has absorbed all of the heavy energy, then you may ask her for her finest living energy to refill your belly-eye. Practice this as long as you need to until you feel your belly-eye is free of discomfort, clean and healthy without any stuck heavy energies.

*\*\*\*NOTE. If you do not feel that you can digest your own heavy energy **DO NOT** attempt to eat the heavy energy of another. Find a teacher to help you. You must be able to eat and digest your own heavy energy before moving to the next step!*

4) EAT AND **DIGEST** THE HEAVY ENERGY ANOTHER PERSON.

Find a partner with whom you feel a very good affinity and who agrees to practice this technique with you. Chose someone with whom you feel your energy Bubble is very compatible, someone with whom you share values, friendship, and a sense of harmony. If you are unsure, close your regular eyes and open your belly eye…perceive the persons Bubble through your Belly Eye and let your belly tell you who is the right one to work with.

Decide between you who will be #1 and who will be #2. Person #1 , you will do nothing at all. Just stand quietly with your feet apart and your body relaxed about two feet away from #2. Person #2, look at your partner like you would look at a DELICIOUS SNACK! Place your hand over your Belly Eye and use your intention to OPEN your Belly Eye by moving your hand further out in front of you. Now that your *Qosqo* is open drop your hand and take a small step forward into your partners Bubble and pull all of their heavy energy into your Belly Eye intending to help them by eating and liberating the heavy energy that is ready to come off their Bubble.

Keep eating until you feel quite full and you know that is enough. Place your hand back over your *Qosqo* and slowly close your Belly Eye. When your hand touches your belly and your *Qosqo* is fully closed take a step back out of your partners Bubble and command your spiritual stomach to **DIGEST**. Notice the heavy energies flowing naturally down your legs and out your feet into Mother Earth. Keep digesting until the downward flow of heavy energy subsides. If you feel the need, open the top of your Bubble and allow the influx of finest energy of the cosmos to help move the flow of heavy energy down your legs and out of your feet. When you feel AS GOOD or BETTER than when you began—you are finished. Thank your partner without talking and relax while #1 returns the favor. Partner #1 will now repeat the exact same steps to eat the heavy energy of #2. When you have finished the exercise of helping each other, thank each other any way you please and talk together about your experiences. You will find that along with your partner's heavy energy you may have received other impressions, messages, images, or sensations. Share those with each other.

CONGRATULATIONS: you have just eaten your first HOOCHA meal. Now...wasn't that delicious? Now at last, you are in an empowered state to help your brothers and sisters. And no you don't need permission to eat a person's heavy energy any more than you require permission to pick up trash off the sidewalk and put it in the dumpster. You cannot take any heavy energy from someone that they are not ready to part with.

PLEASE promise me that you WILL NOT go out the next day

after learning this technique and try to EAT the HEAVY ENERGY OF THE MIDDLE EAST CRISIS! Heavy energies that are collectively created need to be collectively eaten. I'll expand on that idea more in the last chapter of this book.

Please follow these simple guidelines to increase your capacity to eat and **digest** heavy energy in a step-by-step fashion that will not get you into trouble or make you sick. You must make sure to eat within your capacity and not overindulge in heavy energies that have been generated collectively or that you are not ready or capable of digesting.

YEARS of seminars have taught us that if you follow these simple guidelines you will be able to learn this practice without hurting yourself. Start by eating and digesting Bubbles of people that are very similar and compatible with yours. Once you feel very comfortable eating and digesting many Bubbles that are similar to yours--and this could take 7 days, 7 months or 7 years—only then, take the next step. Try eating a Bubble that feels neutral to yours; in other words, a Bubble to which you feel neither attracted nor repelled. Once you feel very comfortable eating and **DIGESTING** many of theses neutral Bubbles you will be ready to move on. You may then try eating and digesting a Bubble that feels very different from yours. Once you have spent a LOT of time eating and digesting Bubbles that feel VERY different from yours, only then should you move on to eat the Bubble of your "arch enemy." This is the capacity you must slowly work toward: that is when you feel completely comfortable to ingest the heavy energy of someone with whom you feel in direct conflict, or with whom you have extremely divergent values or world views. (The Senate should try this!)

Now that we have activated our INKA SEED by performing Hoocha Mikwhee, and warmed the earth of our belly center, it is time for the next step.   On to principle #5!

# CHAPTER FIVE

# SOUL IRRIGATION

## Principle 5.  QARPAY:  IRRIGATION OR ENERGY TRIGGER

**Qarpay literally means watering or irrigation in Quechua.  In the ritual sense it is an energetic transmission of living energy between Nature and humans that triggers our psycho-spiritual growth to the next level.  Qarpay is the irrigation of our Inka Seed that softens the hard outer casing to allow the possibility of sprouting.  The Seven Energy Eyes (Ñawis) of our body open to connect with the five primary living energies of Nature.**

This ingenious system of human spiritual development outlined by the Andean Masters, takes us along a path that requires a step-by-step integration with ever-larger living systems of Nature.  For the Inka, this means an intimate, direct and highly personal process that demands continual shifts in one's very identity.  The germination of our Inka seed begins with an Inka Ritual called *Qarpay.*

Our Inka seed is planted deep within the warm 'earth' of our sacred center, and lies dormant, safe within its hard outer casing, waiting for the right triggers or cues from the environment signaling that it is time to begin to grow.  Then the outer casing of the seed must burst, sending roots down to search for water and sending up a central stalk and unfurling leaves to photosynthesize its own energy. After warming the Earth of our belly by activating our *qosqo* with the practice of *hoocha mikhuy*, the next step is the watering of our Inka Seed. That trigger is called a *qarpay*.

The word *qarpay* literally means 'irrigation' or watering in Quechua. But as you have discerned by now, in Inka philosophy anything that is literal, physical or mundane, also has an esoteric, energetic and sacred significance. *Qarpay*, when used in the energetic sense, means initiation or transmission of power. It is possible, though rare, for a *qarpay* to be given directly from a Nature Being to a student, as in the case of initiation by lightning. More often, the transmission is given from a higher-level initiate to a student.

When you receive a *qarpay* from an Andean Priest, you are receiving the energy of their direct connection to the Forces of Nature. An initiated Andean Priest is called a "*Paqo*" in Quechua and s/he became a *Paqo* through receiving *qarpay*. In other words, *qarpay* is an energetic transmission from the Master directly into the bubble of his/her student. An Andean Priest or *Paqo* is a trained conduit, channel, or delivery system through which the forces of Nature transmit living energy to humans.

A *Paqo* is a conscious voluntary energy transmitter who is empowered to call upon the forces of Nature but the communication goes two ways, meaning that *the forces of Nature may also call upon Paqo*. The *Paqo* serves as a powerful channel of Nature energies to catalyze growth in the initiate. A *qarpay* ceremony can empower your energetic, sacred identity and help prepare your seed for germination. To better explain, I will tell you the story of a *qarpay* I received from one of my most amazing teachers. It happened on my very first trip to Q'ero; a treacherous, at times life-threatening, journey through the rugged cloud-veiled heights of the Andes Mountains.

The year was 1995 and Juan and I were leading a small group of dedicated American *Paqos* to an epic encounter with the Q'ero Nation, the last of traditional Inka villages in the High Andes. We were on a mythical quest to meet the most powerful living priest of the Q'ero Nation, a man who was nearly legend. Miraculous powers had been ascribed to him. He was recognized by all for his amazing healing abilities and for his capacity to speak directly with the forces of Nature. His name was Don Manuel Q'espi. Although his passport read Quispe (a Spanish name with a similar sound) his original Inka name was *Q'espi*, meaning crystal in Quechua.

We had been warned that after all our efforts to arrive to this remote village, Don Manuel might not be willing to receive us at all. Hoping for the best, we had taken a twelve-hour bus ride from hell, then walked or ridden tiny Andean horses along narrow cliff edge trails, through unbelievable mountainscapes, and over dreaded 20,000 foot passes for three days in order to reach the village of Choa Choa.

I must admit the site of the village was anti-climactic after the effort spent to arrive. We shivered in the chill afternoon wind upon sighting the dismal-looking group of stone huts with thatched roofs, huddled together in a dry barren treeless lunar landscape of grey/green rock. Between lunch camp and late afternoon, two guides with several pack-horses had gotten lost, thinking they were taking a short cut through the mountains. There were no roads. With them, went most of our food and camping equipment, and even all of our warm clothes, which we had removed temporarily in the heat of the noonday sun and placed in the horses' gear. As the sun was setting a bitter wind had begun to howl on our arrival to this unlikely place that was home to Andean Master, Don Manuel.

Seeking any shelter from the freezing wind, we dismounted our horses at the nearest empty stone hut where, I unhappily discovered, we had already nearly lost one of our group members to hypothermia. We took him immediately inside and it was only through our collaborative sacrifice of body heat that he was saved as, in desperation, we placed him in the middle of our human body pile to try to jump-start his internal thermometer. A half hour later he was reviving, but still weak, when a messenger arrived with good news. We had been invited into the Community House of the Q'ero Village.

And it was here, as we were recovering with warm tea provided by our unique hosts, that it happened. People had been coming and going through the front door and each time it opened I looked up curious to discover if any of these Q'ero men was Don Manuel…the priest we had traveled all this distance to meet. Then I laughed at myself realizing I had no idea what he looked like.

Suddenly, without any warning sound or movement, all heads swiveled toward the door. The door flung wide and standing before us was a bundle of electrical charge in the form of a diminutive Indian man with cinnamon-chocolate skin and two lighthouses for eyes. These lighthouses swept over us, sizing us up easily with an x-ray like scan. Above his head a brilliant fist-sized star bobbed and weaved as he moved—twinkling with a blue-white shifting light—like a giant diamond. Certain the altitude and trauma had done me in, I squeezed my eyes tight shut and rubbed them. I opened them again. The damn thing was still there. There was absolutely no doubt of his identity.

Don Manuel Q'espi walked straight up to me and challenged,

"I am an Inka come here with the power given to me by God. Who are you?"

Juan translated for me as I squeaked out a pitiful response, yet somehow remained lucid enough to request a ceremony for our group. We were ecstatic when Don Manuel Q'espi agreed to perform a collective offering ritual for us called a "Hayway" or Despacho. A three-hour ceremony ensued during which time our lost pack-horses arrived and we were saved!

The next day, to the amazement and consternation of our well-seasoned guides, Don Manuel offered us his "*qarpay*." This was apparently quite unusual and unexpected. The mountain spirits had given permission for our entire group to receive the *qarpay* of this Master, the direct transmission of his personal power! The experience was so profound and uncanny it was nearly impossible to describe. Only a year later, after hearing Don Manuel's own initiation story, did I even began to fathom what he had actually given or "transmitted" to us.

In the Andes there are four ways one becomes an Andean Priest or *Paqo*. One way is through the family—to follow the path of one's mother, father or grandparents who are already initiated priests and healers. The Q'ero have described to us a process in which the student basically follows their elders around the community helping in a kind of apprenticeship called "servicio" until the day when the student is deemed ready, then s/he receives the *qarpay* of the elders.

Another way is to be called through dreams, illness, or other difficult life experiences. Then if you are lucky and can afford it, you find an Andean priest willing to give you his/her *qarpay*. The third way is very rare. It is when one is struck by lightning. Every single one of these methods involves a *qarpay*, a download of enormous energetic force either coming directly from Nature Herself (as in the lightning strike), or more commonly through an emissary of Nature, an Andean Priest. However, the fourth and most unusual way to reach the Fourth Level is the way of Don Manuel Q'espi. He received his fourth level initiation directly from a being of the *hanaq pacha* or upper world and was known as a special kind of *Paqo* called "*kamasqa.*"

Normally during a *qarpay* ceremony, the priests use a mesa—a bundle of power objects often including rocks—to confer their *qarpay*. The ceremony involves the placing of (or whacking you with) their mesa on the top of your head, while invoking the forces of Nature. The priests are calling on their direct connection to the energetic force of their personal Mountain or Lake Spirit, or, as in the case of Don Manuel, the *hanaq pacha*, the power of the heavenly realm itself.

But this type of power is not given freely; there is always *ayni*, a sacred exchange to be made. Here is the unusual story of how Don Manuel received his fourth-level initiation and became a *kamasqa*.

When Don Manuel was a very young man, about twenty years old, he became extremely ill and was quite close to death. He was bleeding through his male member and no Andean Priest in all the Q'ero Villages could heal him. Desperate, his father told him to go to two of the sacred sanctuaries near Cuzco, called Ocorruro and Wanka. At the Sanctuary of the *Señor de Wanka*, Don Manuel saw a vision of Jesus Christ as an elegant white man wearing gold spectacles, a pin-striped three-piece suit of sartorial splendor, and a gold pocket watch on a chain. Jesus told him he would be completely healed if he went to the Q'ollorit'i Festival (a huge Ice Festival at the foot of a glacier) and made an offering to the spirit of the mountain. Obediently he went to the Ice Festival and once there, saw another vision of Jesus, who told him to go to the top of the ice peak and perform the initiation ritual. Luckily his father was with him and knew how to perform that ritual.

After that Don Manuel had a third vision of Jesus who told him to take a ritual bath in the glacial lakes of Q'ollorit'i and make several offerings. Faithfully he did all those things and Jesus came in a fourth and final vision and told him he had to become an Andean Priest to serve his people, and that he must return three times to Qollorit'i to receive his "mesa"—the ritual power bundle of a *Paqo*. After the final vision of Jesus he returned to his village completely healed.

In an interview with a Canadian journalist Don Manuel told us, "When I had the vision of Jesus I also received the flame of the Holy Spirit in my head and in my body and I was healed. This is why I can speak of these things. If I hadn't received the flame of the Holy Spirit in my head and in my body I could not talk about these things. I could not do the things I can do." This Initiation story defines Don Manuel as a very rare kind of *Paqo* called *Kamasqa*, one who receives the *qarpay* directly from a being of the upper world, the heavenly realm or *Hanaq Pacha*. This "flame of the holy spirit" was the *qarpay*, a direct transmission of living energy from a being of the 7th level, Jesus.

A *Kamasqa* is a *Paqo* who receives initiation into the Fourth Level directly from a Being of the upper world, without any human or Nature intermediaries from the earthly realm of *Kay Pacha*. Due to the syncretization of the Andean tradition with Catholicism and thanks to his Fourth Level perspective, Don Manuel had no trouble receiving his vision from Jesus and using terms like 'the Holy Spirit,' to describe his initiation inside his Nature-Being-filled worldview.

When I received the *qarpay* of Don Manuel nearly sixty

years after his initiation and before knowing any of his story, I experienced what I can best describe as a bolt (or a burning cross) of light entering like fire into the top of my head. That night I had one of the most profound dreams of my life, with an accompanying experience of love and bliss unlike anything I had ever experienced. Another member of our trip described Don Manuel's *qarpay* as "five years of psychotherapy in about thirty seconds." At that time most of us on that trip had little or no idea what a "*qarpay*" actually was. Yet it was clear to us that we had received a powerful energy transmission, and by the law of sacred exchange, when something goes in, something must come out. In this case it was if the *qarpay* of Don Manuel had forced out the old heavy energy clogging up our pipes, our dysfunctional or non-life-affirming patterns of behavior.

Sadly for us all, Don Manuel passed away in December of 2004, yet his spirit lives on in many of his students, quite literally, because we received his *qarpay*.

A *qarpay* is not something that is just given to you. Like all relationships with the energy world, it requires an exchange; you must give something to get something. You may think you know what you are giving, but you never know what you are going to get. Don Manuel had to make a pretty big offering—basically his life—without knowing he would receive his "flame." Normally an initiate in Q'ero has to pay a fortune in cows and sheep, pigs or chickens to receive the *qarpay* of a master. This is a safeguard of the energy world to ensure that you do not receive an amount of energy you are not prepared to handle. You receive according to what you give and in this way you can advance organically along your path.

A *qarpay* can transmit a huge amount of energetic force to potentiate one's bubble, but how we use that potential is up to each one of us. Many are called—few actually answer. Once you answer, according to the Q'ero, you must have a *qarpay* to empower you, to break open the hard casing of your Inka seed and begin the process of spiritual growth.

Anyone who has a Bubble can offer a *qarpay*, but you can only give what you have. If you have received the Fourth-Level initiation you can transmit it to another, but clearly if you don't have it, you can't give it. No one can give initiation into a level unless they are actively displaying that level for all to see. There is no 'faking it.'

Remember, initiation means beginning. Just because one receives the *qarpay* of a Fourth-Level *Paqo* doesn't mean one will automatically arrive to fullness of the fourth level. Reaching the Fourth-Level requires effort and the application of our *MUNAY*. Again, *munay* is a fascinating Quechua term that means love and will working together, similar to Sri Aurobindos' term "love in action."

Since Inka times the Andean Masters have maintained a ritual of initiation into the Fourth-Level that allows one to become a candidate to the fifth level. It is called *Hatun Qarpay* in Quechua or the GREAT INITIATION. This ritual requires the initiate to release his or her old identity, and take on a new identity involving much greater community responsibility. At a certain point in the ritual, initiates enter into a sacred cave to release all the *hoochas* or heavy energies that have accumulated during their lifetimes.

Next, initiates release their identities as the biological son or daughter of their biological parents and receive *INTI TAYTA* (Father Sun) and *Pachamama* (Mother Earth) as their true parents. In this way they redefine themselves, and every human being on earth becomes their literal brother or sister. If one is to come into the full flowering of the Fourth-Level one must manifest this capacity to treat all human beings in this way.

The ultimate practice of *qarpay* is found in the sacred reciprocal exchange of personal power called *QARPAY AYNI*, or, if you will, "mutual irrigation," that happens near the end of the *HATUN QARPAY* INITIATION. We are watering each other's seeds with our own nectars to help each other grow; to empower our collective bubble—what a beautiful image!

There is no *qarpay* without the invocation of Nature and there is no limit to the types and numbers of *qarpays* that can be transmitted. Has Nature been calling you?

The progressive integration with larger systems of nature can go on infinitely; therefore there is no end to the practice of the Initiate of the Andean Path and each instance of practice can reveal new sensations, perceptions, and insights. No two experiences of the Inka practices are ever the same. In my more than twenty years of teaching this tradition all over our fabulous Mother Earth I have received and given thousands of *qarpays*. Each one is completely unique.

When you work with the world of living energies nothing ever 'gets old'. There is no such thing as 'been there done that' because you are working within a scintillating living system that always offers new and unique energies and experiences. In offering the *Hatun Qarpay* (Great Initiation) ceremony in Peru, I have performed the exact same 10-days of rituals more than fifty times and they have NEVER once been the same, because Mother Earth herself is an ever-growing and ever-changing living system.

I feel now, eighteen years later, that I continue to integrate the Fourth Level *qarpay* of Don Manuel Q'espi and for that reason he is still alive in me. Don Manuel taught me that one can only transmit what one has received and there is no way to cheat.

94

If one has received the Fourth-Level initiation one can transmit it to another...but if you do not have the Fourth-Level obviously you cannot transmit it. You cannot give what you do not have. And whatever you have, can and must be given.

If someone tells you they are a master of the Fourth-Level and have received that initiation all you have to do is notice what goes on around them. One cannot pretend to be what one is not because in the Andean tradition your power must be made visible within your community! If you are good at resolving conflicts and creating harmony wherever you go and you are a person that seeks to benefit your community, acting with generosity and love, you are exhibiting signs of the Fourth-Level.

The Andean Tradition provides a great test of the veracity of a teacher's level. If a teacher tells you they are of the Fourth-Level yet is constantly creating conflicts wherever they go, they are exhibiting the behavior of the third level. If the teacher engages in behavior that creates "in group" and "out group" dynamics, or the school has a 'secret inner elite' these are all signs of the third level. You can feel for yourself that those dynamics remind one of high school, the appropriate place for adolescent behavior.

Further if the spiritual training you are receiving involves creating a dependency of any sort between the teacher and the student, this is a third level teacher. For example if you need the 'powerful shaman' teacher to remove the dangerous 'negative entities' that are inside you this is absolutely a classic sign of a third level teachings, because the teaching comes from a fundamentally fear-based model. Also, if someone practices "returning negative energies" to the ones who sent them, they are practicing on the third level. At the Fourth-Level we simply EAT and digest any heavy energies sent to us by others and are grateful for the nice meal.

The Andean tradition also provides a safeguard for teachers and that is called the *Qollana*. *Qollana* means excellence in Quechua and it is the lauded position of the student who always questions the teacher. The *Qollana* is a respectful and dedicated student that is willing to question authority. If you are in a class where the teacher does not respect and invite the *Qollana* type of behavior, or if the *Qollana* is not allowed a place in the class, then you are probably in a third level type system. This would not be unusual as most of the physically adult population of the earth is still living, thinking, and acting at the third level. Again, the third level is not bad, it is not evil - it is simple adolescence.

We are said to have arrived at a great transition of the majority of the world population from the third to the fourth level. Imagine the energetic transformation of the planetary Bubble were a sufficient number of people to shift from third to fourth level! That transformation of Bubbles is considered to be the necessary foundation upon which the next levels can emerge. *Qarpay* is an important trigger for that transformation.

The Andean *Qarpay* or transmission is similar to the *shaktipat* or *darshan* ritual of the Hindu tradition, or what the Tibetans call an "empowerment" ritual. Here is what one Tibetan teacher says about the Tibetan "empowerment:"

> "Our ordinary mind is hard, unripened. So, it must be ripened with the empowerments....While the stream of the nectar is poured into us during the ceremony, we meditate that we transform into the deity state, thereby purifying all our negative thoughts and obscurations..."

### -<u>Lord Jigten Sumgön</u>

There are striking similarities between Inka '*qarpay*' and the Tibetan 'empowerment' ceremonies, as well as the use of the term 'nectar.' However there is an interesting distinction with respect to the focus of our meditation during the ceremony. In the Tibetan tradition one meditates to transform oneself into the "deity state," to purify negative thoughts. In the Inka tradition our practice focuses on the intentional intake of nectars from our highly tangible, visible, and palpable Nature Beings.

## HOW DO WE CONTINUE OUR EVOLUTION TO THE FOURTH LEVEL?

Through understanding and use of the INKA ENERGY SYSTEM we can literally irrigate our Inka Seed with the *sami* or nectars of the *Teqse Apus* and cause our Seed to germinate and grow. Here is a diagram of the Seven Eyes of the Inka Energy System.

# SEVEN INKA ENERGY EYES

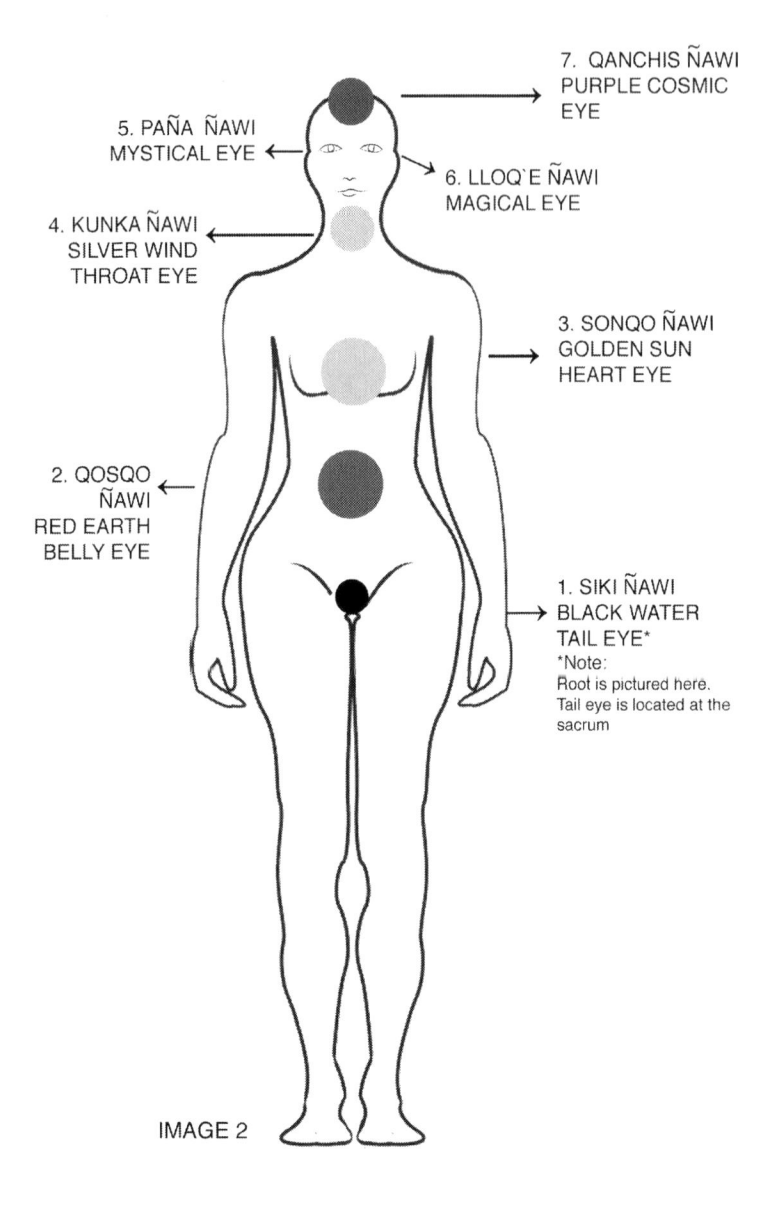

7. QANCHIS ÑAWI
PURPLE COSMIC
EYE

5. PAÑA ÑAWI
MYSTICAL EYE

6. LLOQ`E ÑAWI
MAGICAL EYE

4. KUNKA ÑAWI
SILVER WIND
THROAT EYE

3. SONQO ÑAWI
GOLDEN SUN
HEART EYE

2. QOSQO
ÑAWI
RED EARTH
BELLY EYE

1. SIKI ÑAWI
BLACK WATER
TAIL EYE*
*Note:
Root is pictured here.
Tail eye is located at the
sacrum

IMAGE 2

## The Seven Eyes of the Inka Energy System

Andean Masters teach that we have seven energy "eyes" or centers located at very specific points on the human body, designed as the natural HOMES of the primary forces of Mother Nature. Through receiving the *sami* (nectar) of each of the Global or *Teqse Apus*: Father Cosmos, Mother Wind, Father Sun, Mother Earth and Mother Water, we irrigate our Inka Seed. We are literally opening our 'EYES" to receive directly into our Bubbles the *"qarpay"* of the fourth-level teachers. They are called "eyes" literally *ñawi* in Quechua, because they are doors of perception through which energy can be received and transmitted.

I will elaborate the entire system and then of course I will give you an authentic Inka practice by which you can personally experience this system of living energy for yourself, so you can begin the process of irrigating your own Inka Seed.

Your "eyes" are the natural organ of exchange between yourself and Nature Beings – Mother Water, Mother Earth, Father Sun, Mother Wind, and Father Cosmos. In the Inka wisdom tradition, our health depends upon us forming harmonious relationships with these Nature Beings, and exchanging our energies with theirs. Each of these beings produces a specific kind of Nectar *(sami)*, essential to providing us with the spiritual food that we need in order to grow on our Path. No one would argue that plants require earth, sunshine, air and water to grow. The Inkas teach that we humans also need a steady and varied diet of these precious nectars from Nature.

As we know, for our Inka brothers and Sisters, all the forces of Nature are alive and have a consciousness with which we can communicate. They are not things, not objects, not even 'elements.' We treat living beings in a VERY different way than we treat objects. This is the reason for making this crucial distinction.

In many other traditions around the world, similar Nature forces are called the Five Elements (earth, air, fire, water, and ether – the Inka equivalent to ether being Father Cosmos.) However, the term 'elements' makes them sound like impersonal objects that we can use however we like. Indeed our Western cultural framework says this is so. In grade school we are taught that one of the big developments of our ancestors occurred when 'ancient man harnessed fire.' The Inka point of view differs greatly from this paradigm, as these forces are not elements, but rather beings with their own form of consciousness and deserving of our highest respect.

Our human biologic and energetic anatomy is designed to receive the living energies of each of these "Nature Beings" in a very specific way. Let's examine the Inka Energy Eyes in greater detail.

## TAIL EYE ~*SIKI ÑAWI* ~ Luminous Black Water Eye

The Natural Home of the Mother Ocean and her "water nectar" is in the "eye" or energetic center located at our tail or sacrum. The color associated with Mother Water is luminous black. Think of it as black shot through with gold and silver.

According to this indigenous wisdom system, our sacrums naturally connect to the larger water systems of the earth. Just as the Earth's water systems must flow freely to clean themselves, our energetic and physical health is maintained by the free flow of water sami (finest water energy) into our tails and up our spines and into our brains. This free flow of *sami* carries away heavy energies that can accumulate in the living waters of our bodies.

Let us not forget that we are more than 50% water. From a purely biological standpoint it is interesting that a liquid called cerebrospinal fluid flows back and forth through our spinal cord to our brain by a pumping action located in the sacrum and another in the brain. This cerebrospinal fluid actually removes waste products from our brain. To stay healthy within our bodies this cerebrospinal fluid needs to flow unimpeded from tail to brain and brain to tail.

Luminous black Water nectar feeds our tail and washes away heavy energies.

BELLY EYE ~ QOSQO ÑAWI ~ Red Earth Eye

The Natural home of Mother Earth is in our spiritual stomach, our navel. Let's remember how important our belly button is as it reminds us that this—our very center—once connected us to our biological mother. The umbilical cord is the conduit through which our mother provided us with nourishment. This is the biophilic connection of life between mother and child, and our first connection with 'other.'

Our indigenous informants tell us that we still possess an energetic umbilical cord that maintains our connection with mother earth. This spiritual umbilical cord is never severed. In fact, in order to enjoy optimum health our bellies need to remain or become consciously connected to Mother Earth. As a psychotherapist and more specifically a family therapist, I contend that most Americans and Europeans suffer from "Attachment Disorder" with Mother Earth. It is my fondest wish and indeed my intention that we can heal this 'disorder' causing so much stress, disease, and unhappiness in our modern world through application of the elegant Inka Energy System.

Many report a stabilizing feeling of belonging when they

connect, through the Belly Eye with Mother Earth.

I will never forget my first encounter with Madam Pele, the living spirit of our Big Island Volcano. Pele is the most active volcano in the world. When I first moved to the Big Island of Hawaii, I went immediately to Hawaii Volcanoes National Park in order to pay her my respects. Standing in front of Halemaumau crater, I opened my Qosqo to greet her. The impact of her power literally knocked me to the ground. Laughing, Pele told me, "Now you know why your *Qosqo* is red!"

Neuropeptides found in the brain are also found in the belly, which some scientists say is like a second brain. Likewise, our *Qosqo* or Belly Eye knows things because, according to the Inka, it is the central receptor of living energy of our body. The "belly" is the sacred center within each of that connects directly to the energy of Earth. This is the center from which our Inka Seed will develop.

As our spiritual stomach learns to eat and digest heavy energy, the Inka Seed is activated or "warmed," setting us on our path to the next levels of spiritual development.

Red Earth Nectar nourishes our Belly Eye and stabilizes us by absorbing heavy energies.

Heart Eye - *SONQO ÑAWI* – Golden Sun Eye

For the Inkas, Father Sun is considered an enormously important living being and the true father of all humanity. That is why the Inkas were known as "the children of the sun."

The natural home of Father Sun is in our hearts. We even use language that describes the energetic sensation in our hearts! We all know a 'cold heart' is one that doesn't function well, and that a warm heart is a prerequisite to happiness.

Golden Sun Nectar is the finest living energy of the sun. The practice of receiving golden nectar of the sun into our hearts can cleanse the heavy energy of our hearts that makes us "heavy-hearted." We can help our own heart become like a small sun in our chest, radiating light and warmth out to others.

Did you know that our own sun is a fusion reactor generating clean energy and producing helium? Our sun converts hydrogen to helium at its core. It's a helium factory! When we drink warm golden sun nectar into our hearts we can literally become 'light hearted.' Our sun contains 99.89% of all the mass of our solar system. That is a pretty BIG Dad!

Golden sun nectar warms our heart and burns or transmutes our heavy energy.

Throat Eye ~KUNKA ÑAWI ~ Silver Wind Eye

Our throat is the natural home of the Mother Wind, Mother Moon, and Mother Stars. The silver nectar of these Nature Beings improves our communication, i.e., talking, singing, or speaking. Silver nectar helps us to open our throats to express the truth of our hearts through right speech, songs, stories.

Silver Wind nectar empowers our throat and makes communication flow.

The next two "spiritual eyes" are our actual physical eyes. These eyes function as conduits to certain types of perception, as well as connecting to the purple *sami* of Father Cosmos along with the Seventh Eye.

The Right Eye ~PHAÑA ÑAWI ~is used for mystical and specific perception. It is eye number five. In other words, our Right side and right eye is connected with the mystical aspect of the path—what we consider to be 'left brain functions,'—the logical, rational, cool, organized, methodical, structured aspect of our being. From a biological perspective the right eye sees specifically while the left eye sees holistically, a fact that Hollywood filmmakers have been aware of for decades adjusting their images on the screen accordingly.

The Left Eye~*LLOQ'E ÑAWI* ~ is used for magical and holistic perception. It is eye number sixth. Our left side and left eye is connected with the magical aspect of the path: intuition, impulse, warmth, chaos, wholeness, creativity, healing.

*QANCHIS ÑAWI~SEVENTH EYE*~Purple Cosmic Eye

Our Seventh Eye is our direct connection to the living energy of Father Cosmos. It is located in the center of our forehead above and between our eyebrows, the location often associated with the 'third eye' of the Hindu system. However you will notice that in the Inka Energy System we possess Seven Eyes and when one learns to perceive with all Seven Eyes one becomes what is known in the tradition as *QAWAQ*, a true seer.

Imagine developing your ability to perceive with the full 360 degree perception of your entire Bubble! That is the meaning of *QAWAQ*.

Now you understand the basic mechanics of the energy system that connects us to Nature. ON TO EXPERIENCE!

## NATURE CONTEMPLATION #5: *ÑAWI KICHAY*

## OPENING THE SEVEN EYES

The traditional way to do this practice is to have an Andean Priest place their *mesa* on each eye to help activate and empower this center while also cleaning the *hoocha* or heavy energy found there. But just in case there isn't an Andean Priest handy, you can still do a nice job on your own.

Go outside again to your nice spot on the grassy hill overlooking the lake, river, ocean or downtown central park.

By now you know to relax your body and bring your attention to your physical sensations and then move your awareness to the bubble of living energy surrounding your physical body, which is feeling more refreshed and invigorated than it was before.

Step 1. Bring your attention to the base of your spine and keep your awareness there until you begin to perceive sensation in your 'tail eye.'

Step 2. Apply your intention, your *munay*—the power of love and will together—to open this energetic center like an eye or camera lens, and send your root or long tail out to touch the body of water nearest to you. If you are not near a natural body of water, send your root or tail into the earth seeking the groundwater that is most everywhere beneath our feet.

Step 3. Offer the heavy energy from your tail to the living spirit that is the Water. Most indigenous peoples and esoteric traditions have wonderful names and images for Water Spirits—use any one that works for you. Hawaiians call her "NA WAHINE O KE KAY" the Woman that is the Ocean. The Inkas called her MAMA QOCHA or Mother Water.

Find your personal way to see/feel/sense your connection through your tail to Mother Water.

Step 4. Because you have given, you now have a right to receive the finest living energy of the water—her luminous black nectar.

Receive her Water nectar into your root tail and pull it into your Tail Eye filling and empowering your Tail Eye. Now drink Water Sami through your tail and pull it up into your spinal cord and into your brain, cleansing the cerebrospinal fluid and all the fluids surrounding your brain. Now drink water sami into your heart, lungs, circulatory system, and guts. Take the finest living energy of the water into all the waters of your body. REMEMBER YOU ARE MOSTLY WATER—50 to 60%! Our planet's surface is 71% Ocean. Connect to the living Spirit of Water. Drink and enjoy. Release your *hoocha* to her again and refill with her Water Sami all the places you emptied, practicing your connection. Offer and receive and most of all ENJOY! Mother water washes away hoochas.

We will repeat all four steps with each Eye.

1. Move awareness up to your BELLY and hold your attention there until you begin to feel the sensation in your Belly Eye.
2. Open your belly center like a big eye or camera lens and send a nice thick root or umbilical cord down into the earth from your belly center.
3. Offer any heavy energies that may be trapped in your belly center to Mother Earth and see/feel sense her receiving them. If you wish you can open your Belly Eye and then lie down directly on top of Mother Earth and relax your body into her loving hands and continue your exercise lying on Mother Earth. Mother Earth Absorbs Your Heavy Energies! Take you time. Make the connection.
4. Now you have offered so you have a right to receive the finest RED NECTAR from MOTHER EARTH.

Bring the finest energy of Earth into all the land parts of your body – the organs, muscle tissues, bones, hair, teeth, nails, and skin. Don't forget your skin is your largest organ. Say thank you to all your organs that are always working automatically without us thinking about them. Offer them some gratitude. Release your hoochas and refill all the areas you emptied with Finest Earth Nectar. Mother Earth absorbs hoochas.

NOW move your awareness to the middle of your chest holding your awareness here until you begin to feel the sensation in this center.

Open your HEART EYE, sending a beautiful golden cord directly into the Heart of Father sun. Feel free to offer all of your heartaches, depression, sadness, and heart disease into the center of the sun. Remember, our Sun is 99.89% of the combined mass of our solar system. He's a big guy so don't worry, he can handle it!

When you have released the heavy energy of your heart to the Sun Being, feel free to receive all the love of Father Sun. Receive the golden light and warmth of the sun deeply into your heart. Fill your heart with the golden nectar from the sun. Then spread the finest living energy of the Sun throughout your entire nervous system cleansing every electrical impulse running throughout your entire body. Imagine your blood running gold in your veins and your heart working like a giant golden pump. This is the delicious sun love nectar, coming in to heal you. Take your time. Enjoy this.

Drink until you feel your heart will break…and then drink some more! Release your hoocha again to Father Sun until you feel your Heart Eye is clean, open and empowered. This may take time and a number of practice sessions. Father Sun burns or transmutes hoochas.

Next move your awareness up to your throat area. You may already begin to feel sensation in that area as it becomes ready to open up.

Open your Throat Eye to the Mother Wind and extend a silver web or net out to the Wind from your throat area.
Offer any heavy energy—especially unexpressed words, feelings, or sounds—to the wind. If you wish and you are in a place your feel comfortable make the sounds out loud.

Remember, once you have given you have the right to RECEIVE the silver nectar of the wind into your throat eye. Allow the Wind nectar to flow through your entire Bubble making more space. Offer your hoochas again to the Mother Wind and this time allow your silver net to connect to the Moon and Stars and receive the finest silver living energy from the wind, moon, and stars to fill up your throat eye bringing release and finest energy into your throat area. Mother Wind disperses hoochas.

Now move your attention to your right and left eyes and your 7th Eye. Send a purple beam of living energy into the heart of the cosmos offering any energies or thoughts that need to leave your brain and receive the finest purple nectar of the cosmos into that point and drink it into your brain and into your right and left eyes. Enjoy this connection!

Finally ask the purple sami of your 7th, 6th, and 5th eyes to harmonize with the wind nectar in your Throat Eye, intending that wind and cosmic nectar harmonize in your bubble. Now ask the silver wind nectar to harmonize with the sun nectar in your heart. Now ask sun nectar in your heart to harmonize with earth nectar of your belly and finally ask the earth nectar in your belly to harmonize with the water nectar of your tail.

Now ask all the nectars; Cosmic, Wind, Sun, Earth and Water nectar to harmonize together in your bubble. With all five nectars harmonizing inside your bubble, you may now release through your feet any heavy energies that want to go to Mother Earth. Enjoy this sensation of complete harmony with all the forces of nature inside and outside your bubble.

Notate, draw or record any message, insights, feelings, or perceptions that come to you when you finish this practice.

On to Principle 6!

# CHAPTER SIX

# ENERGETIC GERMINATION

## Principle 6. *WIÑAY*: ENERGETIC GERMINATION

**Our energetic connection to the *TEQSE* (global) *Apus* through our Energy Eyes stimulates the potential of our Inka Seed to germinate. *Chumpi Away* is the Inka practice by which we weave our energy belts to strengthen our Bubble and establish harmonious relationships with our larger natural and energetic environment. We sprout our Sacred Identity by locating and incorporating the natural energies of our *Paqarina* (nature Mom), *Itu Apu* (nature Dad) and Guiding Star. This empowers our Bubble with the requisite living energy to flower forth to our destiny.**

As we participate in the "World of Living Energies" experiencing the forces of Nature as Sacred Beings with their own consciousness that emit living energy, rather than as impersonal "objects," our world becomes infinitely more interesting, we enlarge our family, and much more communication becomes possible. Our Inka Seed has been irrigated with the nectars of the *Teqse Apus* and the sensuous delight of connecting with them may already have caused our seed casing to soften. We begin to experience the benefit of the Inka point of view with no need to abandon our rational logical and scientific perspective. In fact scientific knowledge about Nature only enhances our practice!

Our powers of observation tell us that nature is intelligent, and we are often smart enough to imitate her. The art of making paper came from people watching wasps build their nests. In fact, the entire field of bio mimicry shows how intelligent human engineers observe and copy designs made by Nature—for example the 'Velcro' hook and loop material inspired by cockleburs. If we could but discover the Sun's secret of fusion we could make our own clean energy. Examples are endless because clearly, Nature knows what she's doing.

We have already gotten some practice with connecting to the world of Living Energy and each of the Teqse Apus, ingesting their finest nectar into our *ñawis*, or energy eyes to open our perception. Now let's further explore the worldview that natural forms such as mountains, rivers, lakes, and stars are all living entities in their own right.

The first Q'ero *Paqos* came to the U.S. through Wiraqocha Foundation in September of 1996. One of them was Don Juan Pauqar Espinoza who belonged to a very special class of Andean Priest, initiated directly by lightning. As we were driving across the Golden Gate Bridge to Marin County where he would give his second-ever public lecture, he gazed up at Mount Tamalpais. "What is the name of your beautiful Mountain Spirit?" he asked, enthralled. "She must be very very powerful; look at all the life she has gathered to her, all the people and animals."

From his perspective, Nature is actually the organ of agency and we humans are doing well just to follow along. In the *Inka* view, humans are not *un*important, far from it, but neither are we *all*-important. *We exist as part of a larger system.* We are part of the family of Nature. This is not meant as mere philosophy, but quite literally, as I will explain.

We must now learn that we are intrinsically sacred and

endemically connected to Mother Nature. Allow me to elaborate. If we are part of nature and all of nature, including us, is living energy, what does this mean regarding our human identity?

Sigmund Freud, the "father" of Psychology first defined human identity as an embroiled battle between id, ego, and superego. Carl Jung took us a giant step forward postulating the 'collective unconscious' through his ingenious perception of the similarity in world myth, elucidating a universal source for the structure of the human psyche. Modern Integral Psychology attempts to create an inclusive model through synthesis of world wisdom traditions with modern psychological theory and research.

All of these models rely largely on East/West philosophical and spiritual frameworks that remain stubbornly "human-centric." I contend that Inka psychology elaborates a key 'missing piece' in the puzzle of our human identity, and that key piece is of course, NATURE! Relatively few attempts have been made to integrate wisdom of the North and South and their psychospiritual systems into this model aspiring toward wholeness. What Integral Psychology does offer is validation of an empirical approach based on direct experiential knowledge, which opens the door to the Inka traditional knowledge. What is the basis of our identity from the Inka point of view? Our identity is *sacred, energetic,* and *connected to Nature.*

Jung termed true human development "individuation" and delineated five stages, within a very culturally significant context. Jung said we begin our journey by becoming dissatisfied with the 'persona'—who we think we are supposed to be as defined by society. We then move to stage two, development of the Ego, when we first set out on the journey of true self-discovery by rejecting the persona. The task of Stage 3 is to integrate the contents of our shadow—the part of us that lies in our unconscious—rather than projecting it onto others, thus claiming our own inner authority. Once we are successful we arrive to stage four, the integration of anima and animus, our inner male and female selves. If we can accomplish this sacred marriage we can finally arrive to stage five, our true SELF.

Jung and the Andean tradition help us understand the transition of our current society from level three to level four. I think even Jung might agree that society at large is currently stuck at stage 3, projecting the material of our unconscious onto each other. This is precisely the stage the Inka define as spiritual adolescence. In Jung's model, Stage 4 concerns the integration of anima and animus. This is similar to the Andean fourth level, which is gained through Yanantin, harmonious relationship of complements. As we know, Yanantin literally means "getting married" in Quechua. The Inka tradition continues to describe higher levels that perhaps Jung encompasses in his definition of the 'Self.' But the profound cultural difference between Jung's model and the model of the Inka Masters lies in the basis of our sacred identity.

As with all things Inka, the connection to Nature is crucial and fundamental. And it is there from the beginning, from the moment of our birth. Since for the Inkas and their modern descendants, the Q'ero, everything is part of *"Kawsay Pacha"* the world of living energies—we spring from a living cosmos of ORIGINAL VIRTUE. There is no such thing as Original Sin. Therefore our attitude can ONLY be one of great humility and thankfulness toward the Natural world that sustains us. This sacred relationship must be honored and recognized to maintain the healthiness of our people and our society.

The Q'ero have preserved this viewpoint of their ancestors and live it every day. They enjoy the richness of their worldview and indeed feel great empathy for the pain we experience due to our loss of identity, our loss of connection to *PACHAMAMA*. The Q'ero remind us that rivers and mountains are so much more than our limited viewpoint can comprehend, they are sacred beings and in fact they form a primary part of our very identity. My Q'ero friends were shocked to discover that we were unaware of the information I will impart below, and I feel this is a jewel of understanding so critical to this moment…to discover that we have been living with a human identity that has been missing a solid fifty percent!

## OUR NATURE FAMILY

The Inka masters tell us that we arrive to this world through an energetic door in the sky. Our spirit is attracted to this door, and that door is literally a star in the sky. From our "star door," our spirit (our sacred or energetic self) looks down upon this earth and chooses two human parents to supply our DNA, as well as two Nature parents who will provide us the requisite living energy to accomplish our destiny.

Our Nature mom, *Paqarina* and Dad, *Itu Apu* are the presiding male and female nature spirits at the precise geographic location at which we are born. This spot is literally the place where our spirit makes the irrevocable commitment to our physical body. Our Nature mom and dad form the "spiritual landing pad" of our birth, making the location irresistibly attractive to our human parents.

According to Inka wisdom your spirit is geomagnetically drawn to the location of your birth due to the specific living energies of Your Nature Mom & Dad whose job it is to become your tutelary spirits or spiritual 'parents' for your lifetime.

We must remember that in this point of view everything is alive, including the star through which we arrive to Earth. Our guiding star and our nature mom and dad form a kind of "holy trinity," connecting us with each one of the three levels of the *Kawsay Pacha*, the Living Energy World.

Our guiding star is our personal representative and connection to the Upper World, *Hanaq Pacha*. Our *Itu Apu* is our personal connection and representative in the *Kay Pacha*, the material world. Finally, our *Paqarina* (Nature Mom) is our representative and personal connection with the *Ukhu Pacha* (our inner world or the inside of the earth). Just as Mother Earth reveals precious treasures to those who dig, great treasures can also be found in the Ukhu Pacha (our inner world). Jung would associate the Ukhu Pacha with the unconscious.

Just as your biological mother and father provide you, at minimum, with egg and sperm (and in most cases ethnic, lingual, cultural, psychological, and social heredity as well) your Nature parents provide you with wisdom and most importantly the necessary vital energy for you to carry out your destiny. They also provide a much-needed sense of belonging to a living geography. No matter where you may travel or make your home, they are a source energy for your lifetime.

To be clear, we are not talking about the place you were conceived, or the area in which you grew up. Your Nature parents reside right next to the hospital, house, boat or taxicab in which you were literally born.

It is natural that humans tend to nestle villages at the foot of a protective mountain, close to a lovely and practical water source, often the banks of a river that flows through the valley between the mountains. Our Nature Mom is often (but not always) a river, and our Nature Dad is often (but not always) the mountain that protects the village next to the river.

Your Nature Mom is always a 'female' aspect of nature that exists in very close proximity to your birthplace. She could be a river, stream, lake, spring, valley, cave, or even a mountain!

Your Nature Dad is always a 'male' aspect of Nature such as a mountain, hill, mound, rise, dune, peninsula, or even a river!

We humans have a penchant for naming Nature and we intuitively grasp the maleness or femaleness of various aspects of our geography, which is why Mountains are most often male, yet some Mountains have female names. Many rivers have female names and yet some rivers are male. Still, we tend to think of mountains and hills as generally male, and caves as generally female for obvious rather Freudian reasons. Interestingly, bodies of water are often given female names in many cultures, but not always. The Hawaiians speak of "Na Wahine O Ke Kai" or the 'Woman that is the Ocean.' The Inkas call the ocean Mama Qocha. In almost all cultures Nature is given gender specific names that carry meaning, and for the Inka this extends to the living geography in a very significant way.

In traditional Inka culture, the Nature beings of a person's birthplace are so important and relevant to a person's identity that they often become part of his or her given name. For example, I was born in Manhattan at Mount Sinai Hospital, just a few blocks from the glorious Hudson River. So, according to Inka tradition, my name might be Elizabeth Hudson River Jenkins. Curiously, people often guess I am from New York. This is rather interesting because our family only resided in New York for six months after I was born, and I grew up in Minneapolis, Minnesota.

While we are generally well aware that our human mom

provides us with egg and dad with sperm that allows the creation of the much-studied marvel that is the human body, we are only just now becoming aware of the energetic aspect of our being and its connection to our natural relatives that provide us powerful energetics resulting in character traits and personality quirks that make up what we off-handedly call for example "a New Yorker."

In 2008, one of my most remarkable indigenous teachers, Don Humberto Sonqo Q'espi, dropped an idea bomb that exploded all my previous concepts about healing. He said, "If you are not connected to your *Paqarina* and *Itu Apu* (your Nature Mom and Dad) your power as a healer is ZERO!"

From his point of view our connection to nature is *primary*, whereas for most of us raised in Western culture, Nature is a secondary afterthought, if it is a thought at all.

In this tradition of Nature Mysticism, the art of healing only becomes possible as one transforms into a clearer and cleaner channel or "tube" for directing flows of healing forces from Nature. A healer's value lies in his or her ability to create excellent relationships with the larger forces of nature, in order to call upon and direct these living energies that can actually accomplish the healing process.

Don Humberto Sonqo Q'espi (*sonqo* means heart and *q'espi* crystal) says that we must experience the connection with our *Paqarina* and *Itu Apu* to be fully whole. He then performed a magnificent "Hayway" or 'Despacho' ceremony for each of us to call upon our Nature Mom's and Dad's and thus establish and empower our connection. Of course each one of us first had to identify our *Paqarina* and *Itu Apu* by name.

Take some time to contemplate your Nature Mom and Dad. Google Earth is the *Paqo's* best friend for this research as we can literally lookup the natural features near the homes or hospitals where we were born—but be careful. Along with your brilliant rational mind you must also equally employ your intuitive self to locate and resonate with your own *Paqarina* and *Itu Apu*, and this is a deeply personal process. The absolute BEST way to do this research is to actually go to the place you were born and ask around. You can also find an experienced *Paqo* to help you make an offering, but *you* still have to do the effort of identification and connection.

In the Andes the coca leaf is sacred. Not only is it an amazingly vital source of nutrients but the alkaloids help adapt the human body to altitude (just another gift from mother Nature). Inka priests take three coca leaves together and blow their love offering to the spirits of the mountains. They believe that breath blown with intention directly transmits living energy, like a small offering of love from humans to nature. This small grouping of three coca leaves is called a *k'intu*. *K'intus* work well as a small offering that you can make to your Nature mom and dad, once you discover who they are.

You can then make an offering to call on the living energy of your Nature mom and dad and connect.

As further explanation of this critically important relationship, allow me to share my own personal experiences with my Nature Mom, the Hudson River of New York. Her name according to the Lenape Indians, the Native Americans that once lived on her banks is Muhheakantuk, meaning 'river that flows two ways,' a much more scientific name accurately describing this tidal estuary. Her current name comes from an English explorer named Henry Hudson who "discovered" the river in 1609 as part of an attempt by the English to claim ownership. Whatever we call her, her living energy is the same and I am proud to call her my *Paqarina*.

In 1996, when my first book seemed to have gotten stuck on the publishing conveyor belt, my agent decided it would be a good idea for me to go to New York and speak directly with my editor at Putnam.  Before I left for New York I dutifully made an offering to the Nature spirits of New York city—as required by the Inka tradition—and didn't think further about it.  At that time, I was only vaguely aware of what the tradition said about *Paqarina* and *Itu Apu*, but I had no real experience.  I knew I was headed toward the land of my birth, but I was a 'hiking-boot-wearing-crunchy-granola' Minnesota girl and felt no affinity whatsoever for a big city like New York.

It came as quite a shock when on my first day there, out of the clear blue sky, I heard a commanding female voice in my head say, "Do you really think you can come here to New York City without first coming to see me?"  I had been on my way to the New York Museum of Modern Art when I felt stopped in my tracks.  It was as if the sidewalk had suddenly become a thick mud.  I literally could no longer pick up my feet.

My rational self immediately began wondering if I was losing my mind. Luckily the possibility of conversing directly with Nature wasn't new to me, and I had heard about the idea of the Paqarina and Itu Apu, but had never really considered how it applied to me.  Still, I had some framework to understand what happened next.

The voice told me that she was my *Paqarina* (Nature mom).  "I'm three blocks behind you," she said.  I looked around and saw nothing but city streets.  My rational mind rebelled, and rather than walk in the direction the voice commanded, I went to a kiosk nearby to get a map thinking, "Ok, if she is three blocks behind me then…holy shit! And if she isn't three blocks behind me then…holy shit!"  Either I, or my cultural framework was losing its' mind right there, in the middle of New

York City.

Sure enough the map showed me the Hudson River was just three blocks behind me, invisible due to its steep banks. Giving thanks to my Inka teachers, I put my tail between my legs and humbly went to sit on the banks of my Nature Mom and applied my Inka tools, making her a small traditional offering with flowers and leaves. I blew my finest *sami* with my breath onto the offering and discreetly threw it in the water. She proceeded to tell me precisely why my book wasn't coming out, and explained exactly what I needed to say to my Putnam editor to get the book's publication moving. As it happened she flowed right by my editor's office and could provide me the inside scoop. It was my *Paqarina* that helped my book become published, allowing me to fulfill the next step of what was clearly my destiny.

I took the opportunity of this miraculous communication to ask her if she wasn't choking with the garbage and pollution we humans foist upon her. She answered by offering me a vision of her immensity from headwaters to outlet (about 315 miles) and gently reminded me of her age relative to mine. "When you are gone, I will continue," she told me, righting my puny human perspective in seven words and a picture.

When I continued to question whether New York Mother Earth wasn't suffocating under all those skyscrapers and black top, her answer was clear. "Why do you think New York is such a center of creativity, commerce, business, culture, and art my daughter?" she continued to gently instruct me, "Do you think it is because we Nature beings are weak?" I heard silver peals of laughter. "You humans are drawn here by the energetic power of our beings…and YOU reflect OUR natures." As in many of my encounters with Nature Beings, I had my perspective given a sharp 180-degree twist.

It took longer for me to encounter my *Itu Apu,* aka, the living spirit of Great Hill, Central Park West. I didn't have my first real physical encounter with him until last year in 2012 and I am still digesting the power of that experience that was revelatory. As a result of my own personal experience I cannot stress enough the importance of going to visit your *Paqarina* and *Itu Apu* physically, whenever possible.

If you are lucky enough to live near your *Paqarina* and *Itu Apu,* go there and make an offering and receive a gift for your *Mesa* if you have one. It will transform your healing practice.

If it takes you some time to truly encounter your Nature Being parents, don't feel rushed. Just know that they are there, giving you energy and support.

In the Inka viewpoint, your nature Mom and Dad are just like parents or perhaps grandparents…they are wiser, older, have a huge accumulation of knowledge, a much deeper and wider perspective, and are sought for guidance on any major move in your life. They are loving and generous and charged with guiding us on the path, but like good kids we have to show them respect and honor as well. It's a two way street. Their living energy and guidance is key to accomplishing our destiny.

In the mid 1700's before the arrival of Captain Cook and European disease, Native Hawaiians could chant their ancestors back thirty generations. They knew stories about their lives and descriptions of what they looked like. They were not just reciting a list of names, but invoking a sense of identity and a stream of living energy connecting them to their lineage -a lineage consisting not only of people but of the natural beings, the intelligence of the land. Native Hawaiians call the Hapuu Fern and the Koa tree their relatives. They are the body forms of the

Goddess Hina, a physical manifestation of a Nature power. They are relatives.

For the Q'ero it is nearly inconceivable that we did not know about where we came from, about our connection to our guiding star, *Paqarina* and *Itu Apu*. They could never have imagined that we needed this to be explained. Yet once we communicated this gap in our education to Don Humberto Sonqo, one of my most powerful teachers of the healing arts of Q'ero, he understood precisely. Don Humberto told us that one of the biggest problems he finds in his healing work with the people of our culture is their disconnection from their *Paqarina* and *Itu Apu*. In the healing sessions he performs with his wife and healing partner, Doña Bernardina, all over the world, they almost always need to call for the *Paqarina* and *Itu Apu* of the patient to come back and reconnect.

For him the only power of a healer is the power to act as a conduit for the forces of Nature. "What am I," he told us once, laughing, " but a big sack of *hoocha*." He went on to explain that it is only through our connection with the Nature beings that we become effective healers.

The Q'ero have told us many times that they developed their form medicine for the simple reason that they have nothing else! "There are no hospitals in Q'eros. We can only pray to Pachamama and the Apus for healing."

Let me repeat that in this tradition of Nature Mysticism, the art of healing only becomes possible as one transforms into a clearer and cleaner channel or "tube" for directing flows of healing forces from Nature. In this point of view, people as separate individual human beings are not really good for much as healers. The goal is to create excellent relationships with the larger forces of nature, so that one might call upon and direct these living energies that can actually accomplish the healing process. To regain our connection to our *Paqarina* and *Itu Apu* is key to our societal healing. It is certainly much more difficult to throw toxic waste in a river you consider your Mom, or blow a hole in your Dad to put through a highway.

Many of us may have trouble considering the idea that we chose our human parents. It is usually considered a lucky (or unlucky) accident over which we have no control. What would it mean if we did indeed choose our parents, and that we choose not only two but FOUR?

When we die we give our physical body back to Pachamama and exit in our Bubble through our 'star door'. Interestingly enough Pacha means "world" or more precisely "time and space;" and Mama—well, we all know what Mama means. So "Pachamama" literally means "our mother in time and space," suggesting that were we NOT in time and space, perhaps we would have another mother.

If we truly choose to connect to the living energy of our Guiding Star, and our Mother and Father Nature beings, what would be different? Certainly just thinking about it might give you a feeling of greater support, an enlargement of your family. What would that mean to our everyday lives? Let's try it and find out.

Don Humberto Sonqo Q'espi says that we must perform a ritual of *QARPAY AYNI*, an exchange of personal power, with our guiding star. We must offer all our personal power, meaning all of our love, intelligence, and physical power, and put ourselves at the service of our guiding star. Once we do this we have a right to ask our guiding star to bless our *Itu Apu* and *Paqarina*. Our guiding star then offers energy to our *Paqarina* and *Itu Apu*, and they in turn offer their energy to us, in a great triangular *AYNI*. We can then receive the original energy from our *Paqarina* and *Itu Apu* to complete our Bubbles.

For now, take a moment to think about this. How many of you already feel an affinity with a certain star in the sky? How many of you already know your star? How many have already felt a guiding hand, a helper? Perhaps you call it by a different name; our higher self, spirit guide, or ally.

Even if you don't know who your human parents are, you still have their DNA. The same is true with your star. Your Bubble is still energetically connected to your star even if your brain doesn't know which one it is. Your Bubble knows. Trust it.

Since everything happens through reciprocal exchanges, try the Inka Practices 1 & 2 again but with this variation. Once you have received the nectar of the Cosmos, offered your heavy energy to mother earth, and then received her finest energy back up into your bubble, add all your love. Offer your finest nectar directly to your guiding star. Use your *munay* to direct your living energy through the power of your intention. You have given so now you have the right to receive. Now receive directly back into your bubble the living energy of your personal guiding star. Fill your bubble with this delicious nectar and drink it into every cell of your body and every elementary particle of your bubble and release your *hoocha*. Enjoy this.

Now using your *MUNAY* offer again all your finest energy to your Guiding Star and ask your guiding star to bless your *Paqarina* and *Itu Apu*. Then receive the living energy of your *Paqarina* and *Itu Apu* directly into your bubble to complete your energy.

Your *Paqarina*, *Itu Apu*, and guiding star are like the

'holy trinity' of your energetic identity, your sacred self. Ask your guiding star to help you find your *Paqarina* and *Itu Apu*, your Nature being mom and dad. Your Bubble knows. Trust it.

Those who have worked with the Q'ero may have seen them blowing three times on their *k'intus* (coca leaf offerings). They are delivering the *sami* of their *Munay, Llank'ay* and *Yachay*; heart, body and mind, to the *Apus. K'intu's* work well as a small offering that you can make to your Nature mom and dad, while you are asking them to speak to you, once you realize who they are. Bay Laurel is used by many *Paqos* in the mainland US as a replacement for the coca leaf. You can make a *k'intu* of Bay Laurel and then call on the living energy of your Nature mom and Dad first offering to them in the spirit of sacred reciprocity.

Just as in adolescence we often reject our parents, many of us, especially in the U.S., might feel a kind of dissonance with the place of our birth, and consequently with our *Paqarina* and *Itu Apu*. It is only when we begin to truly practice at the Fourth Level that our perspective becomes large enough and mature enough to integrate the power of our Nature Parents. It is now, at the Fourth Level, when we take on our own inner spiritual authority, that our real independence, maturity and the call of our destiny comes into play.

You may or may not feel an instant affinity with your *Paqarina* and *Itu Apu*, just as we often need to reject our parents as a natural step of adolescence. However, you can be sure once you are able to integrate the living energy of your Nature mom and dad, you are beginning a whole new era on your spiritual journey toward fulfillment.

The reclamation of our Nature mom's and dad's is another one of the great treasures the Q'ero offer us from their knowledge trove about our direct and intimate connection to

Nature. Now I wish to offer you some amazing stories the Q'ero shared with us rather recently, that further elucidate their enthralling mystical worldview.

In mid-September of 2011 Juan Apaza Flores, son of Don Mariano Apaza, spent two months at my house in Hawaii, bringing along his two children Rina Marta and Ruben and two more girls - their cousin Aurelia, daughter of Don Francisco Apaza, and Karina Sonqo, granddaughter of Don Humberto Sonqo and Doña Bernardina. The children attended school with my two sons.

With the help of Fredy Conde Huallpa, a Native of the town of Lares and an excellent Quechua to English translator, we recorded the following story. We asked Juan about a mystery that had puzzled us for many years. Why was it that Fredy (a capable and Native speaker of the Quechua language) often could not understand the rapid-fire prayers of the Q'ero Priests during despacho or *qarpay* ceremonies?

Juan explained using a metaphor we could understand. "You have your ATM card from the bank," he told us, "which has its secret code that you must put in to withdraw money. When we receive our Initiations, the *Apus* (mountain spirits) give us prayers that are like sacred codes to open and call on the energy of the mountain spirit. Those who are given sacred codes by the Apus—(incomprehensible prayers of great beauty) can entice the forces of nature to come. That is why we are able to give transmissions of energy from the Apus. Without these sacred codes we would not be able to do what we can do."

Both Fredy and I were delighted by the clarity of this explanation. But Juan had more to tell us.

"Back in the days of the old and very powerful *Paqos* of

Q'eros," he continued, referring to the 1950's and 1960's, "there were *Paqos* who could do amazing things. There were Paqos that knew the sacred codes to open the door in the mountain of Q'eros. When they invoked the prayers that opened this door, a guide would come and take them into the Heart of the Ausangate Mountain in five minutes."

Needless to say our jaws dropped. Normally, traveling from Q'ero to the heart of the Ausangate Mountain, a snow peak of more than 22,000-ft. elevation, requires a hike of more than six days!

"These *Paqos* would enter a beautiful tropical garden in the heart of the Ausangate Mountain where every food was available in abundance, and from there they would cut the bamboo for their *Pincuyos* (traditional Q'ero flutes)," Juan continued. The story was strikingly similar to Tibetan accounts of visits to Shambhala, a temperate oasis in the midst of a glacial mountain peak.

"How do you know? Who told you this?" we asked, our jaws hanging open in incredulity as he related his story with the serious ingenuousness of a Q'ero.

"My father told me, and he knew these *Paqos*. He heard the stories from them himself. He saw the bamboo they brought back." Juan's father was the famous *Paqo*, Don Mariano Apaza.

Of course we had to ask, "Are there any *Paqos* now who know the sacred codes?

"Sadly not," replied Juan, shaking his head. "But my teacher Don Manuel Q'espi always told us that we must keep practicing our tradition because one day in the future there will once again be *Paqos* that will receive this knowledge and know how to make the *Apus* and the *Pachamama* speak."

Well aware that there had been a lot of contamination of the Q'ero Tradition since it began to gain enormous popularity in early 2000, I knew it was best to wait until I had received a second independent verification of this unique and exciting story of Juan Apaza. The confirmation came in June of 2012. While I was traveling on a teaching tour with Don Humberto Sonqo and his wife Doña Bernardina, I took the opportunity to casually mention the story.

"Yes of course," Don Humberto confirmed. "Everyone in Q'ero knows that in the hillside behind the blue lake of Q'ero there is a door in the mountain that can be opened if you have the sacred codes," he said. He was even able to detail the precise location of the doorway. Unfortunately, Don Humberto also confirmed that there wasn't a single living priest in Q'ero today who knew the codes.

During the 1955 expedition to Q'ero, Oscar Nuñez del Prado recorded many of the myths kept faithfully through the oral tradition of the Q'ero Priests. It could be from this first expedition or later ones that there is mention of a sacred city known as *Miskayani*. This etheric sanctuary is described as a place of infinite peace and prosperity ruled by highly evolved female priestesses possessing profound wisdom and knowledge of the healing arts, as well as unparalleled beauty and a deep sensuality. The Q'ero men to this day speak of Miskayani with rapturous longing and an intense desire to attain the purity to be allowed entrance into the city. While the Q'ero women, if they speak at all, speak of the danger of attempting the journey. In Q'ero and even in the Cuzco area, one can hear many stories of farmers coming out of the jungle with an ear of corn made of solid gold, and legends of a fabulous city with every kind of food, gold and precious materials. While Miskayani remains a little-known myth shrouded in mystery this female sacred city, like all things Inka, has her male counterpart—which is very well known indeed.

Paititi is the basis for the myth of "El Dorado", a legendary "lost city of gold" in the Peruvian jungle. Like Miskayani it is thought to be a city of pure gold, perhaps through a conflating of spiritual riches with material ones. However, the "El Dorado" tale has mostly come to signify the search for an incredible treasure trove of gold. The story is so well known that Disney has even made a movie of it called "El Dorado." Since the 16th century numerous Spanish expeditions have been undertaken to locate the whereabouts of "El Dorado" in order to claim its treasures. Later, in 1911, the same year that Hiram Bingham, the National Geographic Explorer, was credited with the 'discovery' of Machu Picchu, another explorer, Colonel Fawcett, was hot on the trail of "El Dorado." His was one of the most well-known expeditions as the man appeared inhumanly impervious to jungle diseases. Yet he too succumbed, as so many others, and mysteriously disappeared never to be heard from again. Since Colonel Fawcett's time there continue to be countless expeditions launched to locate the mysterious lost city to this day! Over the past five centuries, hundreds, perhaps thousands, of explorers have been lost in the jungle, never to return from their search.

While Paititi is a well known tale, *Miskayani* seems a land yet undiscovered, it gives one the sensation of a story as yet to be revealed. I first heard about Miskayani in 1996, when Wiraqocha Foundation brought Don Manuel Q'espi out of Peru for the very first time. Invited by Stan Grof, Don Manuel was one of the Key Note Presenters at the 25th International Conference of the Association of Transpersonal Psychology in Manaus, Brazil. We had quite a time actually getting Don Manuel to the conference, as we had to file three lawsuits in the city of Cuzco just to get him his passport!

Once he finally arrived to the lobby of the Hotel Tropical Manaus, we invited him to come and greet the Rio Negro River, which flowed right past the hotel. Don Manuel immediately got out his pouch of coca leaves and began making a *k'intu*, offering his *Munay, Yachay,* and *Llanqay* on his breath to the spirit of the river. We watched him in awe as his bubble grew and grew in a manner that was tangible as he connected to the river and received her power in return. As he turned around to face us with the most incredulous smile on his beaming face, he said "we must be very close to the borders of *Miskayani* here because there are so many hundreds of ñusta's!" For him (and any Q'ero male) the Ñust'as are very sexy, nubile female nature beings and his face revealed his surprise and enthusiasm at their presence.

According to the Q'ero expert Juan Nuñez del Prado, the name *Miskayani* refers to "the tender sweetness of the newly germinated plant." *Miskayani* is a great treasure and source of healing power as the *Ñust'as* of *Miskayani* are said to be most powerful healers. *Miskayani* signifies another *yanantin*, the creative power yet supreme tenderness of the newly germinated plant. Now is the perfect moment to move on to the practice of *Wiñay*; Germination.

HEALTH, HARMONY, and HAPPINESS are the natural by-product when we practice making the harmonious relationships with our natural and energetic environment required for germination. We proceed with our evolution through the seven levels of psychospiritual development contained within our "Inka seed," by applying the five nectars to weave our energy belts to strengthen and empower our bubble and sprout our Inka seed. Germination unfurls our stalk and leaves through which we can gather the requisite energy to continue the journey of our spiritual evolution, the ever-deeper interpenetration with Nature's larger systems.

To help us better understand here is a diagram of the Inka Energy Eyes and Roots, and the Four Energy Belts of the Inka Energy System.

# CHUMPI AWAY
# WEAVING THE ENERGY BELTS

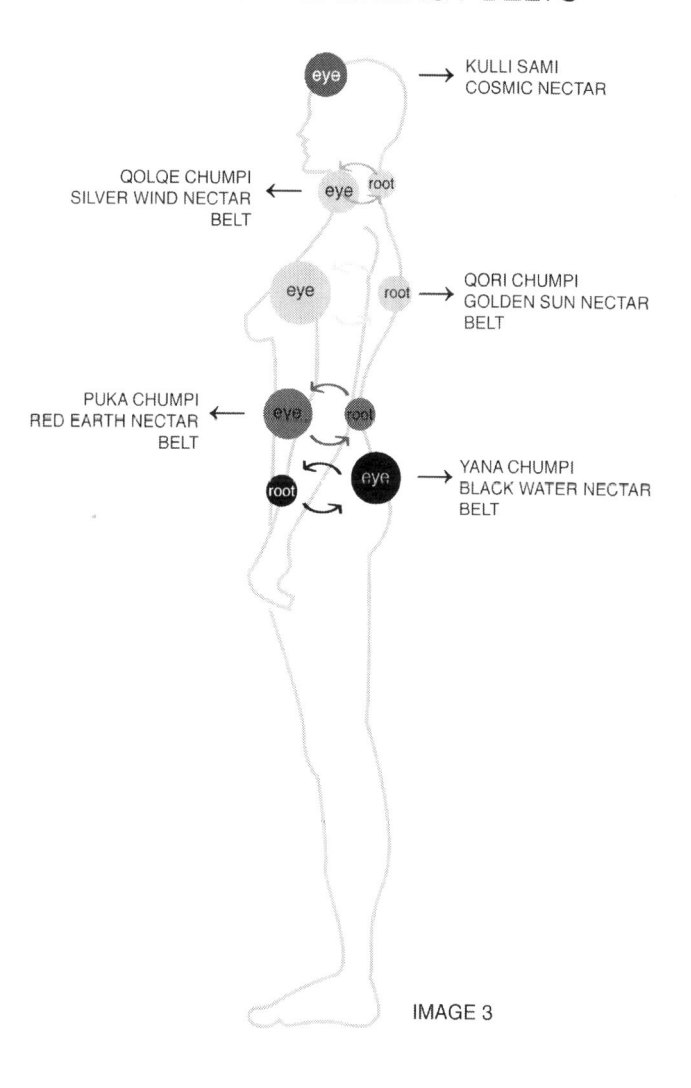

KULLI SAMI
COSMIC NECTAR

QOLQE CHUMPI
SILVER WIND NECTAR
BELT

QORI CHUMPI
GOLDEN SUN NECTAR
BELT

PUKA CHUMPI
RED EARTH NECTAR
BELT

YANA CHUMPI
BLACK WATER NECTAR
BELT

IMAGE 3

# NATURE CONEMPLATION #6: *WIÑAY &*

## *CHUMPI AWAY*

## Germination & Weaving the Four Energy Belts

This is the next practice of the Fourth Level initiate. It is a practice of the spiritual irrigation of the "eyes" and activation of the belts with the five "nectars" to produce germination of your Inka Seed!

Find your nice quiet space where you won't be interrupted. This practice normally takes about 20 minutes.

Bring your awareness to your breathing--your sacred exchange with the plants. Enjoy this until your awareness naturally flows to your Bubble. Open the top of your Bubble and receive finest energy of the Cosmos. Open the bottom of your Bubble and offer your heavy energies to mother earth and feel the connection through you to Earth and Cosmos.

Receive finest energy of Mother Earth in sacred exchange and offer all your nectar back to the Cosmos and your guiding star. Offer the *sami* of your guiding star to your *Paqarina* and *Itu Apu* and then receive their power.

By doing this you are creating a complete link between you and your personal representatives in Heaven (*Hanaq Pacha*), Earth (*Kay Pacha*), and your Inner World (*Ukhu Pacha*).

Now bring your attention to the base of your spine until you feel a tingly sensation there. Open your tail eye and extend your long tail or root down into the nearest natural water body -maybe the groundwater beneath you.

Make a sacred gift of all your heavy energies from your tail to the living spirit of the water and feel them flowing out of your tail into her hands. Once the outflow has subsided, ask to receive the finest living energy...the nectar of the water spirit...the 'black light.'

Enjoy this delicious finest water energy flowing into your tail center and filling your tail eye and root. Now continue to pull the water sami, filling your tail eye until it is overflowing.

Apply your *Munay* to weave together your Tail Eye and Root using the luminous black nectar, empowering your black belt as it naturally begins to form and flow around your sacral area. Offer your finest Sami back to the water spirit and receive her finest luminous black energy again filling your black belt with a lovely sensuous flow of pure water nectar.

Enjoy your powerful connection to the Mother Water and the circulation of your black belt. Enjoy this experience.

Now bring your awareness to your Belly Eye. If you wish, lie down directly on top of Mother Earth and Open your Belly Eye and send your energetic umbilical cord down into Mother Earth. Allow all of the heavy energy from your Belly Eye and root to flow out your umbilical cord and down into Pachamama.

Once you feel this outflow has subsided you have a right to receive because you have given. Receive the finest red nectar of Mother Earth drinking it up into your umbilical cord and into your Belly Eye connecting you intimately with this source of Mother Earth food coming into your belly. Now Fill your Belly Eye to overflowing with Red Mother Earth Nectar and use it to weave together your Belly Eye and Root forming the natural red *sami* belt that begins to flow around your waist area.

Enjoy this delicious stability and security of your red belt connected and circulating around your waist and back and forth between you and Mother Earth. Send your finest nectar, your Sami, back to *Pachamama* through your energy umbilicus and perceive how you are viscerally intimately and personally connected to the land beneath through your red belt. Enjoy.

Now move your awareness to your Heart Eye. Open your Heart Eye and root and send your golden cord into the heart of Father Sun. Offer any sadness, heartache, loss, fear, anxiety offer any and all the heavy energies from your heart into the very heart of Father Sun. Especially send the heavy energies from your root, the space behind your heart...any pain from the past...offer this directly into the heart of Father Sun.

Now that you have given you have the right to receive. Receive the golden nectar from the heart of Father Sun directly into your heart, filling you with warmth and love, and the fresh clean finest living energy of the sun. Receive the love of *INIT TAYTA*, Father Sun, and allow your heart to warm and even heat up with golden Sun nectar until it is overflowing.

Now using the golden Sun *sami*, weave your Heart Eye and Root together forming the natural golden belt that flows circulating around your torso. Fill up your entire golden belt with warm golden Sun sami. Circulate golden Sun nectar back and forth with Father Sun through your golden belt and enjoy the connection.

Now bring your attention to your throat eye. Offer all the unspoken or misspoken words, your screams your shouts offer all your heavy energy from your throat eye and root to MOTHER WIND, and send it out like a silver net or web, streaming out in all directions from your throat eye and root.

When the outflow of heavy energies has subsided, receive the pure silver nectar from the Mother Wind coming in to enter your Throat Eye to overflowing and use the silver Wind nectar to weave together your Throat Eye and Root circulating fresh silver wind nectar and connecting your silver belt all around your throat 360 degrees.

Offer your love to the Mother Wind, Mother Moon, and Mother Stars and Receive all their silver nectars into your silver belt and circulate it until you feel harmony in that area. Now circulate silver wind nectar back and forth with Mother Wind, Mother Moon and Mother stars through your silver belt. Enjoy this sensation!

Bring your attention to your right and left eyes together with your 7th eye and send a purple beam of light into the heart of Father Cosmos offering your purest love into the heart of our living Cosmos. Now that you have given you have a right to receive. Receive the finest energy of living Cosmos the purple nectar from Father Cosmos…let it fill your eyes and your mind and refresh your thoughts transmuting any doubts or fears with pure finest cosmic nectar. Allow your mind to fill with the infinite power of the cosmos and enjoy.

Now from your Seventh Eye use your munay to send this purple nectar down the central channel of your body and allow it to flow into your Inka seed located just inside the central channel between your tail and belly eye. Feed the purple cosmic nectar from its' source directly into your Inka Seed. Feel the tingling power of your silver belt connected to Wind, Moon, Stars and send the silver Wind nectar into your Inka Seed. Next feel the warmth of your golden belt and feed the golden Sun nectar to your Inka Seed. Send the Red Earth Nectar from Pachamama through your red belt to empower your Inka seed. Now send the luminous black water nectar through your black belt into your seed. Feed each nectar to your seed until you feel your seed crack or pop open in germination.

Now ask all the energies of Mother Water, Mother Earth, Father Sun, Mother Wind and Father Cosmos to harmonize together in your Bubble and release any heavy energies out your feet and into Mother Earth that are now ready to leave your Bubble. Give thanks for this beautiful experience and when you feel very harmonized and VERY grounded softly open your eyes maintaining the sensation, the harmony of your bubble connected with all the living energies of Mother Nature and with your belts energized. Take a few minutes to notate your experiences, insights...write or draw them. Notice how you feel now compared to how you felt before you began this practice.

ON TO PRINCIPLE #7

# CHAPTER SEVEN

# SPIRITUAL FLOWERING

## Principle 7. PHUTUY: ENERGETIC FLOWERING

**Culmination of our Fourth-Level practice occurs through the nourishment of our Inka Seed and sacred identity, with the living energies of the Five Nectars to bring about spiritual 'flowering.' This prepares us to practice the ultimate *Qarpay Ayni* that marks the beginning of the collective energy practices. We continue our evolution through the seven levels of psychospiritual development that take us on a journey of ever-deeper collaboration with Nature's larger living systems.**

> *"A human being is a part of the whole, called by us the Universe, a part limited in time and space. We experience ourselves, our thoughts and feelings as something separated from the rest—a kind of optical delusion of consciousness...Our task must be to free ourselves from this prison by widening our circles of compassion to embrace all living creatures and the whole of nature in its beauty...We shall require a substantially new manner of thinking if humankind is to survive and evolve to higher levels."*

> *-- Albert Einstein.*

My heart is open wide as I write this chapter because at the end of it, I will offer with you my very favorite of the Inka Practices, called *flowering*.

The Inka, geniuses at recognizing and imitating natural structures, observed that the human physical body possesses the same energetic structure as the body of Mother Earth as a whole. The Earth, too, has a spiritual center. Like our own sacred center or belly eye, this area has the power to eat and digest heavy energy. And so the Inkas designed their cities, from Q'eros to Cuzco, imitating the same energetic structure they observed in the human body, the geography of the land, and that through modern science, we find present today in structures from cells, to humans, to Earth, to solar system, to galaxy.

The Inkas created their cities following the precise energetic structure they found in the human and animal body with seven energetic ñawis or "eyes." Cuzco city is laid out in the form of a PUMA honoring *Kay Pacha*. At the tail of the Puma located at the bottom of Avenida Sol, you will find a large and beautiful water fountain erected to honor the Spirit of water. This fountain is the *siki ñawi*, water tail eye, of the city. The *qosqo ñawi*, earth belly eye, can be found at the Qorikancha temple, the place where Inka Priests ritually "ate" and digested the heavy energy of the city and even the whole Empire. The sun heart eye, *sonqo ñawi*, is located at the main square that in Inka times was much larger and was named "Rejoice." The wind throat eye of the sacred city, *kunka ñawi,* is found at the Palace of Manqo Qapac in San Cristobal once you climb the street called 'Pumas' Shoulder.' And the fifth, sixth, and seventh eyes are located at the Head of the Puma in *Saqsaywaman*.

Machu Pikchu is laid out in the shape of the hummingbird honoring *Hanaq Pacha* and each of the seven eyes or energy centers can be found in the temples of Machu Pikchu, just like in Cuzco. The temple of Wiraqocha located in Raqchi, contains the energy form of a serpent honoring the *Ukhu Pacha* and the ancestors. Wiraqocha temple lies South of the Cuzco, on the road to Lake Titikaka and the Tiwanku culture. The Inkas are thought to have ancestors from both Wari and Tiwanaku culture and Wiraqocha Temple is considered an archaeological link to Tiwanaku.

In the early 1400's Wiraqocha Inka, the Eight Sapa Inka who ruled with Qoya Mama Runu, is credited with the transformation of the Inka religion to monotheism by devotion to the one metaphysical God, Wiraqocha. He thus earned his name, Wiraqocha Inka, after having a vision of this unlimited spiritual being Wiraqocha—literally meaning 'the living energy behind all manifested form.' Wiraqocha Inka built a temple to honor this being that can still be seen today in the village of Raqchi. Through his spiritual visions Wiraqocha Inka gave a prophecy that the Inka Kingdom would reign for five more generations and then the Inka people and their religion would disappear from the earth. It is said that Inka Wayna Capac, grandson of Pachacuteq, died with that prophecy on his lips after his division of the Empire between his two sons, Waskar Inka and Atawallpa, led to the civil war that facilitated the Spanish conquest of the Inka Empire.

It seems uncanny that after hearing such a prophecy, the son of Wiraqocha Inka, Pachacuteq, would go on to build what was perhaps the largest subcontinental empire on Earth. Scholars argue whether Inka Pachacuteq rejected the prophecy of his father, or whether his adamant desire to preserve Inka culture actually fueled his gargantuan expansion project, transforming tiny kingdom into subcontinental Empire. Despite his efforts, the Inka Empire did fall in five generations just as Inka Wiraqocha predicted. However, its spiritual traditions did not disappear from the Earth.

In the lineage of the last Priest-King, Sapa Inka Waskar, Don Benito Qoriwaman was considered one of the last great Fourth-Level Andean Priests of the Cuzco Valley and a veritable treasure trove of Inka wisdom. Much of Don Benito's wisdom is expressed here in this book due to the enormous generosity of one of his principle students, anthropologist Juan Nuñez del Prado. Juan is the son of Oscar Nuñez del Prado, leader of the 1955 Q'ero Expedition, and undeniably the worlds' foremost authority on the Q'ero people, outside of themselves of course, and the Andean Mystical tradition.

Don Benito was concerned about the potential loss of his tradition and, as a true Fourth-Level Master, looked for students capable to carry the knowledge forward. He recognized Juan as one of his foremost students who would help with the preservation of the Inka tradition, and trained him alongside another mestizo, Americo Yabar. Don Benito charged Juan with teaching and sharing the tradition with others. Juan does so, thereby maintaining the vitality of the sacred places through their continued traditional use, as well as exemplifying one of the chief Inka virtues - generosity. He has been teaching and sharing the Inka tradition since the late 1980's.

Among some of the most important things passed on to Juan by Don Benito was the *Hatun Qarpay,* or Great Initiation of the Inka. This is the ten-day ritual of initiation into the Fourth-Level, allowing one to become a candidate for the Fifth. Before Don Benito died, he was able to guide Juan through the first day of the ritual, and to describe the rest in enough detail for Juan to achieve its complete resurrection, which he did in the early 1990's.

The ritual of *Hatun Qarpay* takes the initiate on a journey of deep immersion into the sacred geography of the Cuzco and Machu Pikchu areas, culminating in the coronation ritual of the Inka performed on the penultimate day, at the ancient temple of Wiraqocha. As with all things Inka this—ten-day, twelve hours per day—ritual requires innumerable exchanges of living energy between these magnificent Inka sacred sites and human initiates. It also requires twelve *Paqos* initiated into the Fourth-Level. Don Benito's concern for the loss of his tradition was well founded, because upon giving Juan the ritual in 1987 he stated that there hadn't been enough Fourth-Level Paqos to perform it for the preceding fourteen years. The *Hatun Qarpay* (and specifically the coronation ritual within it) requires a minimum of twelve Fourth Level *Paqos*. Each one must energetically connect with one of the twelve *Panakas* or Inka Royal lineage temples at the sacred complex of Wiraqocha in the town of Raqchi. Performing the *Hatun Qarpay* keeps the ancients sites activated and healthy and is an important responsibility of the *Paqo*.

One of the first stops on this ten-day ritual of Hatun Qarpay is *Saqsaywaman*, a magnificent ruin that lies on a hillside overlooking Cuzco city. The name comes from the ancient words *Saqsay*, meaning Puma and *uman* meaning head. The area literally forms the head of the puma that is the ancient Inka capital of Qosqo. The design and building of this temple with its miraculous 'organic architecture' in the Imperial style is attributed to Inka Pachacuteq and therefore, the walls are said to be imbued with his power.

If you visit this ruin you will see three walls that zigzag along the top of the mountain made of enormous stones weighing up to *20 tons* each. That is 40,000 pounds! These stones are carved and set in place with such precision that not a hair can be inserted between them, and they fit together like perfect puzzle pieces without the use of mortar of any kind. In fact, these stone walls, inserted more than two meters deep into the ground, lie on top of enormous rounded boulders set beneath them that provide the wall the unique feature of flexibility. This is a highly practical function considering the high frequency of earthquakes in the area. These Anti-seismic walls that modern engineers, even today with all our modern technology, cannot replicate, supply us a hint into the depth of practical knowledge and intelligent collaboration with nature this civilization and its millennial spiritual tradition possessed.

If you observe the design and placements of the walls you will see that all of the 'organic architecture' of the Inkas follow the lines of Mother Nature. The hillside is not cut or blasted away to put up the human wall, the natural flow and shape of the hillside is preserved, humans emphasizing and following the lines created by Nature. There is no denying the Inkas had a deep respect for the genius of nature and enough human intelligence to follow her lead. In fact I contend that Machu Pikchu is above all else a monument to the collaboration of Human and Nature intelligence, and that this collaboration produces a *sami* finer than Nature or Humans can produce on their own. Machu Pikchu is pointing the way to our future.

As with its architecture, every practice for human growth follows the genius of Nature and all metaphors for human development take their imagery from Nature. So, naturally, the Inka framework for spiritual development begins with a seed and culminates in flowering. As there are individual flowers that make a garden, there are collective flowerings. All of the Inka Rituals are considered to be collective spiritual work, as the Inkas were a society unparalleled in social organization that mastered the gathering and redistribution of resources both physical and energetic to benefit the whole.

At the Fourth-Level any power sought or insight gained by an individual is only important if it is shared to benefit the community. That is why in this tradition there is no going off to a cave by oneself to meditate; the spiritual practices are always performed in community. The only possible motive to gain personal power or achieve enlightenment is so that it may be shared to benefit the whole. In fact the very meaning of personal power in the Andes is defined as "what you can do." In other words if you claim to have a power, it means absolutely nothing until is has been demonstrated in a way that benefits your community. Therefore becoming a human conduit of the forces of Mother Nature is the highest path, as she is clearly recognized to be the biggest power.

Up to now we have discussed in detail only the transition from the Third to the Fourth-Level of psychospiritual development according to the Inka system. We know directly about the first four levels from current Andean masters living in modern times up until the late 1980's, who were master healers or masters of the weather. Don Andres Espinoza of Q'eros and Don Benito Qoriwaman of Wasao elaborated these levels in all their detail to their students before they died in the 1980's.

You can meet Don Benito Qoriwaman in Shirley MacLaine's book, *It's All in the Playing,* published by Bantam in the same year Don Benito died, 1987. Although she mistakenly calls him a "brujo" which means sorcerer, rather than affording him his proper title of *Kurak Akulleq* (meaning highest Fourth-Level Inka priest) she offers us a beautiful window into her experience with this unequalled Master of Andean wisdom.

In chapter 21, she explains how Don Benito made a special offering (despacho) for her, then taught her how to use it to hold back the rain in Machu Picchu in order for her ABC film crew to get their footage. Ms. MacLaine was actually trained to work weather by one the greatest Andean Masters of the twentieth century, and for his immortal presence in her book, I am forever grateful.

In my lifetime I have known only four Q'ero *Paqos* of the

fourth level. Now there is only one remaining Q'ero master of the Fourth-Level alive today who still lives in Q'ero, and is recognized as a *Kurak Akulleq* by all the Q'ero community. Here is a diagram of the higher levels and further discussion about the qualities of these levels.

# LEVEL 5, 6 & 7

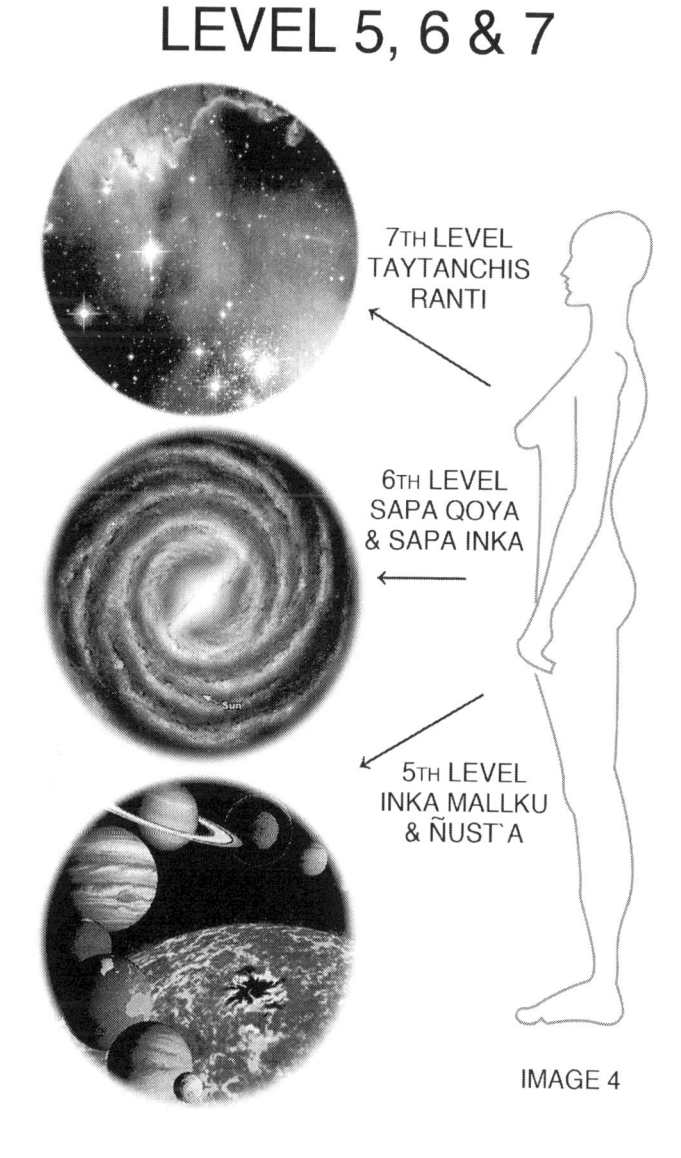

7TH LEVEL
TAYTANCHIS
RANTI

6TH LEVEL
SAPA QOYA
& SAPA INKA

5TH LEVEL
INKA MALLKU
& ÑUST`A

IMAGE 4

We have had no known initiates higher than the Fourth level living in the twentieth and twenty-first centuries.

What we know by description is that the Fifth Level initiates, called *Inka Mallkus* (male) and *Ñust'as* (female), are ultimate healers and possess the capacity to heal every illness every time through one single touch. Another capacity of the Fifth Level initiate is that by their simple presence alone, they bring the energy of resolution. In other words if a Fifth-Level initiate walked into the United Nations, the power and influence of their Bubble would instantaneously initiate creative solution sessions to conflicts between peoples of all nations present.

Many other spiritual traditions speak of people of this level having walked the Earth in earlier times. I have personally heard stories from Native teachers of the Hawaiian, Native American, Toltec, Mayan, and Tibetan traditions that tell of such people. No doubt there are more. Christ was certainly considered to have demonstrated the healing power of the Fifth-Level more than two thousand years ago. Yet it is astonishing to think that this level was said to have been present in the human population during the Inka Empire, less than five hundred years ago!

At present, we know of many healers with great abilities, but none who can heal every illness every time with only one touch. The reason invariably given for the inability to heal the person is that they must learn some lesson through their illness.

Thus I suggest that the re-appearance of the Fifth-Level in such capacity as the Inka Prophecies outline, signals a transformation of human society and that perhaps we will have arrived at a new a stage of human collective development. This level would be one in which the focus of our human evolution necessitates resolution of collective rather than individual *hoochas* or 'karmas' if you will.

Following the model given by the Andean Masters, the fifth level would correspond to a person who has the capacity to resonate their bubble with the next larger Natural living system; and that would be our solar system.

The capacity of the Sixth-Level is said to be the level of the Sapa Inka and Sapa Qoya—the High King and High Queen of the Inka Empire. These people are considered to be truly enlightened leaders of such power, integrity, goodness, that is to say, of such spiritual quality and evolution that they literally glow or shine with their own light that everyone can see.

Inka Pachacuteq, the ninth Inka ruler, was said to glow when he exited the *Qori Qocha* (golden lake) where he had gone to pray with Inka Priestess Chanan Qori Coca for guidance on how to defeat the Chancas.

The story goes that in 1438 the Chancas, archrivals of the Inkas, had attacked the sacred city of Qosqo. The reigning eighth Sapa Inka, Wiraqocha, was said to have abandoned Qosqo leaving it undefended. His son, young Prince Cusi Yupanqui, refused to abandon his city, but at seventeen-years-old he did not have the power to make his people follow him. He asked the High Priestess Chanan Qori Coca what to do and she took him to a sacred lake and told him, "Pray to the God of your father, pray to Wiraqocha." He entered the lake and prayed as Chanan Qori Coca instructed him. When Prince Cusi Yupanqui emerged from the lake glowing with a light everyone could see, the people rallied around the young leader and it was said, "even the stones stood up and became soldiers fighting under his command."

For his deeds Prince Cusi Yupanqui earned the name Inka Pachacuteq, meaning 'world transformer' or literally 'world turned upside down.' *Sapa Inka* Pachacuteq and his *Sapa Qoya*

Mama Anawarqe with their descendants expanded the Inka realm from a little kingdom of no more than 25 miles around Cuzco city, to one of the largest sub-continental Empires on earth. The capacity of the Sixth-Level (Sapa Inka & Qoya) is thought to correspond to the ability to resonate ones' Bubble with the energy field of our Milky Way galaxy. Arguably one gains the capacity of a black hole, to eat and emit light.

The capacity of the Seventh-Level is termed '*Taytanchis Ranti*' which in Quechua means, "equivalent of God on earth." The Seventh-Level initiate is said to have complete mastery over matter, and to be able to resurrect their physical body from death. Certainly the story of Jesus' resurrection would qualify him as a Seventh-Level initiate. The capacity to resonate ones Bubble with the entire energy field of the universe is considered to define the Seventh-Level, and this capacity is said to exist within every human being in the form of the Inka Seed.

While these higher levels are somewhat speculative given that they were not specifically described in modern terms of solar system, galaxy, universe by the Andean Masters; nonetheless it is remarkable that our South American brothers and sisters have conceived such a vast and far-reaching spiritual system. Since these levels are universal, and once we understand the qualities of each level, we can recognize them as existing in many cultures worldwide. Though these higher levels may seem way out of reach, we must remember that levels five and six are said to have been present during the Inka Empire, less than five hundred years ago.

The Inka spiritual systems emphasize a fascinating point, that with each advance in levels, each expansion of the energy field brings new solutions to problems that are not available from the perspective of the previous level. It is important that we enlarge our vision, and literally our energy field, to find solutions to our problems at hand.

Now it is now time to flower!

This is the practice that allows you to increase your capacity
to resonate with the entire energy Bubble of Mother Earth, and to
augment the capacity of your bubble to reach the full flowering of
the Fourth Level.


## NATURE CONTEMPLATION #7: PHUTUY

### Flowering or The Teqse Paqo Contemplation


Bring your awareness to your breathing--your sacred exchange
with the plants- and enjoy this until your awareness naturally
flows to your bubble. Open the top of your Bubble and receive
finest energy of the Cosmos. Open the bottom of your Bubble
and offer your heavy energies to Mother Earth and feel the
connection through you to Earth and Cosmos. Receive finest
energy of mother earth in sacred exchange and offer all your
nectar back to the Cosmos and your guiding star. Next offer the
*Sami* of your guiding star to your *Paqarina* and *Itu Apu* and then
receive the living energy from your *Paqarina* and *Itu Apu*,
creating a complete link between you and your personal
representatives in Heaven (*Hanaq Pacha*), Earth (*Kay Pacha*),
and your Inner or Under World (*Ukhu Pacha*).


Now bring your attention to the base of your spine until you feel a
tingly sensation there. Open your tail eye and extend your long
tail down into the nearest natural water body....it may be the

groundwater beneath you, or it may be your *Paqarina*. Make a sacred gift of all your heavy energies from your tail to the living spirit of the water and feel them flowing out of your tail into her hands. Once the outflow has subsided pull into your tail eye and root the finest living energy of the mother water…the nectar of the water spirit. Fill your black belt with finest luminous black light Sami and enjoy this delicious energy circulating around and empowering your black belt. Once you feel the black belt is filled up with Finest Luminous Black Water Sami, Offer your finest nectar back to the water spirit and enjoy your powerful connection to the Mother Water. Notice how your belt and tail is connected to the water spirit, and how her body is connected and flowing into other water bodies. Let yourself expand, flowing along her body connecting to the stream or river or lakes nearby. See how they flow together and connect you to your very own *Paqarina* and feel how your *Paqarina* is connected to all the rivers, lakes and mighty oceans of our Mother Earth. Experience how all the waters of your body are connected, flowing and resonating in synchrony with all the living waters of our entire Planetary Body. Feed the Nectar of the *Teqse Mama Qocha*, the Global Mother Water, to your germinated Inka Seed. ENJOY!

Keeping your tail immersed in the water, bring your awareness to your Belly Eye and send your energetic umbilical cord down into Mother Earth. Allow all of the heavy energy from your Belly eye and root to flow out your umbilical cord and down into Pachamama. Once you feel this outflow has subsided receive the finest red nectar of Mother Earth drinking it up into your umbilical cord and into your Belly Eye and connecting and flowing into the Red Sami belt that forms around your waist. Enjoy this delicious stability and security of your red belt connected and circulating back and forth with Mother Earth. Send your finest nectar, your Sami, back to Pachamama through your umbilical cord and perceive how you are viscerally intimately and personally connected to the land beneath you through your red belt. Notice how the pachamamita just beneath your feet is connected to the other pachamamas next door, and they are connected to the Pachamamas of the towns and cities all around you. Now feel all of the country you live in as one being connected to you, and feel how your country Pachamama is connected to all the other Mother Earth Spirits of all the other countries in each continent of the world. Expand your experience of connection until you can feel all the lands of Mother Earth connected and resonating through you and to all the land of your own body. Feel yourself as all of Pachamama. Now offer this finest *sami* of all of Pachamama to your germinated Inka Seed. Enjoy this connection.

Keeping your tail in the water and your belly in the earth, move your awareness to your Heart Eye. Open your Heart Eye and send your golden cord into the heart of Father Sun. Offer any sadness, heartache, loss, fear, anxiety offer any and all the heavy energies from your heart into the very heart of Father Sun. Now that you have given you have the right to receive. Receive the golden nectar from the heart of Father Sun directly into your heart eye and root filling up your golden belt with warm golden sami, circulating sun nectar with Father Sun and enjoying the connection. Feel the entire power of Father Sun inside your chest as if Father Sun is literally shining inside you. Feed this delicious golden sami to your germinated Inka seed. Enjoy!

Now keeping your tail in the water, your belly in the earth, and your heart in the sun, bring your attention to your Throat Eye. Offer any heavy energies that might be in your throat to the Mama Wayra...mother wind. When the outflow of heavy energies has subsided, receive the pure silver nectar from the

Mother Wind coming in to enter your throat eye and root, and fill up your silver belt all around your throat 360 degrees. Offer your love to the Mother Wind, Mother Moon, and Mother Stars and Receive all their silver nectars into your silver belt and circulate it until you feel connected with Mother Wind, Mother Moon and Mother Stars. Feed the silver sami to your germinated Inka seed. Enjoy this sensation!

Continue to keep your tail in the water, your belly in the earth, your heart in the sun and your throat connected to Wind, Moon & Stars, and bring your attention to your 7th eye and send a purple beam of light into the heart of Father Cosmos offering your purest love, your nectar, into the heart of our living cosmos. Now that you have given you have a right to receive. Receive the finest energy of living energy cosmos the purple nectar from Father Cosmos…let it fill your eyes and mind refreshing your thoughts. Allow your mind to fill with the infinite power of the cosmos.

Now from your seventh eye use your munay to send this purple nectar down the central channel of your body and allow it to flow into your germinated seed growing a luxuriant stalk up the central channel of your body. Feed each Nature nectar to your plant, allowing it to grow stronger, taller unfurling leaves as it grows higher up your central channel.

Now ask your plant what it needs to bloom…more Water? Earth? Sun? Wind? Cosmic Sami? Feed as needed until you produce a beautiful bud at the top of your head. If it wishes to, allow your bud to bloom and open into its' fullness. Notice the shape and color of the petals, smell the fragrance of your flower.

Finally, ask your beautiful flower what it needs to fill with nectar.

Before completing the exercise make sure to ask the purple

cosmic Sami to harmonize with the silver wind Sami, and the wind Sami to harmonize with the sun, sun with earth, and earth with water. Then release any *hoochas* through your feet.

This contemplation can release new layers of hoocha from your bubble so make sure to open your feet and release any hoochas completely so that you feel very grounded.

When you feel a beautiful energized harmony in your whole bubble and completely present and grounded with Pachamama, softly slowly open your eyes.

Please take a moment to notate, draw, or sing your experiences.

## THE STORY OF THE CONDOR

## AND THE HUMMINGBIRD

One day the hierarchy of birds had gathered in the meadow. Everyone was there: the Kestrel, the Falcon, the Owl, the Condor, and the Hawk. The Condor bragged to the other birds that he had taken a great flight, the longest, highest and farthest ever, and had come to the very gates of the Upper World. At that moment the Hummingbird arrived saying, "That is true brother Condor, but I have flown beyond the gates to the very throne of God in the center of *Hanaq Pacha*." With the other birds as witnesses the Condor and Hummingbird made a bet, each claiming that they could fly to the center of *Hanaq Pacha*.

On the appointed day all the birds gathered again in the

meadow but only the Condor appeared. They waited, but the Hummingbird was nowhere to be seen. The other birds required that the Condor still attempt the flight, albeit alone, because 'a bet is a bet.' Not one to back down, the Condor raised his great wings and made a magnificent flight stopping to rest at the very border of *Hanaq Pacha*. At that moment out sprung the Hummingbird from his hiding place in the feathers of the Condor and flew to the very throne of God in the heart of *Hanaq Pacha*.

This Andean metaphorical story teaches us that we need the strength and power of the Condor to achieve greatness. The Condor, symbol of the collective Andean People's is also the greatest of *Hoocha* eaters amongst animals, cleaning death away in the great recycling of Nature. However one must combine the Condors' power with the intelligence and joy of the Hummingbird to arrive to the throne of God in the Heart of *Hanaq Pacha*. The nectar of our flowers attracts the hummingbird from the center of *Hanaq Pacha*. Once we have gathered enough nectar in our flowers, we entice the hummingbird to come and drink, and this moment embodies the Andean concept of the moment of enlightenment. In another meaning, even enlightenment is a collective work between the Hummingbird and the Condor.

One of the meanings of collective work at the fourth-level in the Inka culture has to do with their view of competition. An Inka custom says that if two Indians meet each other on the road and challenge each other to a race up the mountain; whoever wins the race is obligated to offer to teach or train the other in his winning methods. This philosophy applies to group competitions as well and ensures the uplifting of the collective to the highest level through the required sharing of best practices. It is the precise opposite of our current corporate model of competition that strives for the advancement and enrichment of the few at the expense of the collective.

All of the Inka practices explained here in this book can be performed individually or as a collective exercise. The performance of a collective ritual is defined by the Inka word *Pukllay*. *Pukllay* (pronounced poohk-lee-eye) literally means ritual or 'sacred play.' It is fascinating to note the recent research on the critical importance of play in human development. The joy of play certainly characterizes the personality of the Inka Mystical Tradition. The ceremonies of the Q'ero are always carried out with a healthy dose of playfulness along with profound invocations of gratitude that bring tears and laughter together all in a natural flow. The seriousness of self-importance disappears I find the collective rituals to be the most exciting, energizing and rewarding as we can easily find a way to remain individuals while working together in a spiritual and energetic collaboration with our beloved Mother Nature.

Let me offer some examples. The first exercise of *saminchakuy* can be performed in a group with these simple instructions. After practicing *saminchakuy* individually, you then receive Sami into your Bubble making it gloriously fat and full until it is literally touching the Bubbles next to you. Next allow the edges of your Bubbles to melt bringing your awareness into the group bubble. Now using the power of your collective intention you can receive Sami together into your group Bubble, and release your collective hoocha to Pachamama. This generally gives a very amplified experience of the individual exercise and bonds the group energy together, empowering everyone.

Each of the seven Contemplations with Nature has a collective form of practice that I promise to describe in detail in my next upcoming book. This book will provide detailed explanations and instructions for the '*hayway*' or '*despacho*' ceremony, the traditional offering made to keep the *AYNI* with Mother Nature, as well as the traditional Q'ero structure and use of the *Mesa*, the *Paqos'* power bundle of sacred stones. The *despacho* is the oldest form of conflict resolution in the Andes, and the *mesa,* like the *despacho,* is the tool of the *Paqo* for performing healings, calling on help from *Pachamama* and the *Apus,* and literally helping to create the energetic connection with Nature beings for performing *Qarpay* ceremonies to water our Inka Seeds.

Here at the final chapter of this book and its final practice we make a complete circuit back to the very first practice teaching us humans how to learn the dance of elementary particles....TO EXCHANGE LIVING ENERGY! By this practice we learn to OFFER EVERYTHING WE HAVE and to RECEIVE EVERYTHING ANOTHER HAS TO OFFER US. We must become totally active (like Father Sun) and give everything, then become totally receptive (like Mother Earth) and receive EVERYTHING rejecting nothing. This is done through a reciprocal exchange of personal power called *QARPAY AYNI.* Here at the final chapter of this book and its culminating ritual we are practicing the ultimate energy exchange.

The great thing about a *Qarpay Ayni* ceremony is that its goal is for everyone in the group to share power, share knowledge, to potentiate equally the Bubble of every *Paqo.* We grow the capacity and bravery to 'give everything away' in order to 'receive everything anew,' and this is done with the goal to potentiate the collective field of the group. To be capable to give and receive equally requires a high level of trust! It's also a lot of fun, and a beautiful and sacred experience. *Qarpay Ayni* is known as the ritual of BECOMING EQUAL as through intentional Bubble exchange in a group, we enhance the collective field; we share all our power with everyone.

This practice exemplifies the Andean philosophy of generosity and collective work. Rather than dragging everyone down to our lowest collective level, we are helping to elevate everyone to our highest level.

With the Qarpay Ayni we bring humans back to doing what elementary particles do to **generate** quantum fields...EXCHANGE ENERGY! This is the meaning of the most fundamental initiatory practices of the Fourth-Level and as always; the highest level involves the simplest ritual.

Prior to performing a QARPAY AYNI with another person, we advise you to receive the Qarpay of an initiated Fourth Level priest, or if there isn't one handy, to practice Nature Contemplations 1-7 together.

First practice *saminchakuy* together to receive cosmic nectar in the top of your bubble and release your heavy energy, with each of you is paying attention to his or her own personal bubble. Then practice *saywachakuy* together, receiving the nectar of mother Earth, adding your finest living energy (your nectar) and sending that back to the cosmos. Then offer your nectar to your guiding star, ask your guiding star to bless your Nature Parents and receive their nectar into your bubble and release your heavy energy. Next go back to back and circulate earth and cosmic nectar together using the Inka Practice of *Yananchakuy*, then you are ready to eat each other's *hoocha*. When you have opened your seven eyes and empowered your bubble with the *TEQSE APUS* the Fourth-Level Nature Being Teachers, germinated your seed, activated your belts, and have performed the flowering contemplation, you are now ready to perform a very powerful Qarpay Ayni

Throughout this book each of the previous Inka practices has been preparing you and your Bubble for this moment, so that you are able to perform *Qarpay Ayni*, or mutual irrigation. I repeat, since this is the MOST powerful ritual of the tradition, and so it is also the simplest. The secret of giving good QARPAY is to KEEP IT SIMPLE. You are not performing a healing or doing any other thing. You are completely focused in giving away all your power and then receiving all the power of another. You are performing a *Qarpay*. That is all. IT IS VERY SIMPLE.

It is traditional to offer a *Qarpay Despacho* before performing *Qarpay Ayni*. If you know how, do it, and if you haven't learned that yet, no worries!

## QARPAY AYNI: Exchange of Personal Power

## a.k.a., Mutual Irrigation

THE STEPS:

1) Decide who will give first--the other will receive. Then both of you may wish to call on *your Paqarina, Itu Apu* and Guiding Star and whatever other teachers or guides you wish to help empower you and prepare you to give and receive.

2) GIVER you will focus your awareness in your bubble and use your *MUNAY* to fill yourself with your own personal power. You may do this by remembering a powerful experience or simply intend that you completely fill yourself with ALL of your personal power. You can call your *Paqarina, Itu Apu*, guiding star, allies, spiritual teachers, or whatever you do to fill yourself with your own personal power. DO NOT DOUBT. DO NOT BECOME DISTRACTED. If you doubt you are transmitting Doubt *Qarpay* rather than your personal power. REMEMBER, you are calling all this power to you so that you can offer, literally give ALL OF IT to help empower the Bubble of your friend.

3) RECEIVER you are using your *munay* to open your bubble to the maximum and become fully receptive to the deliciousness you are about to receive.

4) GIVER you then place both your hands over the fontanel (hairline) of your partner without physically touching them, and apply your *munay* (love and will) to transmit all of your power, all of your nectar, all the best of you, directly into their bubble. This is simple and takes about sixty seconds. When you are finished put your hands down.
DO not put your hands anywhere else. This is *QARPAY*. You are simply transmitting into their Bubble and trusting their Bubble to deliver the energy appropriately.

5) GIVER you will now receive and RECEIVER you will now give. When you have finished thank each other and share your experience together.

CONGRATULATIONS. You have now just done what any good elementary particle in the quantum field does every day. Notice how do you feel…. has your perception shifted? Write down or draw or sing or dance any of your new insights. WELCOME TO YOUR NEW LIFE. You are now part of the system…. THE ECO SYSTEM!

"QARPAY SHAIKU INKA MUJUTA" means, in Quechua, "we are watering each other's Inka seeds." This is the song we sing for fun and beauty after performing a *Qarpay Ayni* ceremony. You can download this song in Quechua if you wish, along with the Nature Contemplations.

The great thing about the *Qarpay Ayni* ritual is that, once you know how to do it, you can perform this exchange of personal power with anybody that has a Bubble! And that means just about everybody: humans, animals, storms, rivers, clouds, stars, and rainbows. Using our *munay* we can offer all our power and receive all of their power in a perfect reciprocal exchange! In this way we are aiming our intention in a biophilic or life affirming direction.

Here at the end of this book, you have no doubt personally experienced that you can create a more healthy, happy and harmonious you by using these simple but powerful Nature Contemplations. Through the practice of *saminchakuy* and *saywachakuy* you can cleanse and ground your bubble everyday. By connecting with your Guiding Star, *Paqarina*, and *Itu Apu* you can feel more energetically supported and centered in your Sacred Identity. By eating the heavy energy of yourself, your friends, family and community, and practicing *yananchakuy* you can create more harmonious interactions with others. By cleansing and empowering your Seven Eyes with the *Teqse Apus* to practice germination and flowering you can become more empowered by and connected to your environment, literally transforming yourself into an 'energy ecologist.'

Once you try these Inka practices, there is no going back, because the result of the practice is its own reward. The trick is to remember to use them when you need them because once you release your heavy energy, you can feel so much better that you actually forget you ever felt bad. That is why I encourage a daily practice.

CONGRATULATIONS AGAIN!

You have now successfully completed the first seven foundational practices of the Inka Nature Wisdom Tradition. You have also joined a new family. You will find that the World Wide *Paqos* of the Andean Tradition are a lot of fun, and have the most ridiculous senses of humor! You are welcome to join our annual meeting, which happens somewhere in the world on or near the Summer solstice.

You can also look forward to my next practical books about the tools of the Inka Tradition. Please see our website for my other books and/or further information on seminars, trainings, or Initiation Travel in Peru or Hawai`i. You can also find out how to contribute to any Wiraqocha Foundation Project, such as the Q'ero Kids Education Project, Q'ero Women's Health Project, or to our new High School of Spiritual Arts (a kind of real Hogwarts for kids.) With a wide open heart full of tropical Sami,

Elizabeth

# Author Bio

Elizabeth B. Jenkins, M.A., MFT, is a farmer and author of three books on Inka Nature Wisdom. *The Fourth Level, The Return of the Inka,* and *Journey to Q'eros.* She is a sought-after public speaker and teacher, and travels extensively throughout the world. She lives with her partner Barney and their two sons on an organic farm on the Big Island of Hawaii where she farms, writes, and conducts intensive workshops and seminars. She is the Founder Director of Wiraqocha Foundation with a mission to bring people and Nature together through education, service and *sami.* For more information please see us on the web.

www.thefourthlevel.org and

www.wiraqochafoundation.org

See you there!